WHEN THE LIONS CAME TO TOWN

The 1974 Rugby Tour to South Africa

LUKE ALFRED

Published by Zebra Press
an imprint of Random House Struik (Pty) Ltd
Reg. No. 1966/003153/07
The Estuaries No. 4, Oxbow Crescent, Century Avenue, Century City, 7441
PO Box 1144, Cape Town, 8000, South Africa

www.zebrapress.co.za

First published 2014

1 3 5 7 9 10 8 6 4 2

Publication © Zebra Press 2014
Text © Luke Alfred 2014

Photographs:
Cover © Getty Images/Allsport
p. 71: © Wessel Oosthuizen, *Vaderland*, June 1974; p. 127: *Rapport*, 23 June 1974; pp. 131 and 136: Danie Craven, *The Legends of Springbok Rugby: Doc Craven's Tribute* (Howard Place: KC Publications, 1989); p. 133: © Gallo Images/ Sunday Times/Avusa; p. 185: © Colorsport/Colin Elsey

Every effort has been made to trace copyright holders and to obtain their permission for the use of copyright material. The publisher apologises for any errors or omissions and would be grateful if notified of any corrections that should be incorporated in future reprints or editions of this book.

All rights reserved. No part of this publication may be reproduced, stored in a retrieval system or transmitted, in any form or by any means, electronic, mechanical, photocopying, recording or otherwise, without the prior written permission of the copyright owners.

PUBLISHER: Marlene Fryer
MANAGING EDITOR: Robert Plummer
EDITOR: Bronwen Leak
PROOFREADER: Ronel Richter-Herbert
COVER AND TEXT DESIGNER: Jacques Kaiser
TYPESETTER: Monique van den Berg
INDEXER: Robert Plummer

Set in 11.5 pt on 16.5 pt Adobe Garamond

Printed and bound by Interpak Books, Pietermaritzburg

ISBN 978 1 77022 653 1 (print)
ISBN 978 1 77022 654 8 (ePub)
ISBN 978 1 77022 655 5 (PDF)

Contents

WHEN THE LIONS CAME TO TOWN

Acknowledgements

Three men, two of whom watched the 1974 Lions tour live, were of invaluable assistance in helping me write this book, clearing up facts and providing me with fresh information and insight. John Griffiths, the English rugby historian, was remarkably generous with queries and historical morsels I would not have been able to find elsewhere. He has a wonderful memory and was able to provide answers to some deeply trivial questions like: 'What is a Welsh love spoon?' Herman le Roux, the former rugby writer and sports editor of *Volksblad* was unfailingly polite and similarly helpful. He allowed me access to his scrapbooks, notebooks and cuttings files and dealt with any number of questions. A hearty thanks to both of you. Mike Shafto, who covered the tour for *The Star* and was the ghostwriter of Willie John McBride's local newspaper column, was another great help. We had numerous long telephone conversations, particularly in the planning and early stages of the book. You were always a source of inspiration, Mike. It was no different this time.

Words of considerable thanks must also go to Albert Grundlingh, head of the history department at Stellenbosch University. Albert was always on hand to open the SA Rugby archives at the university for me – and have a burger and beer afterwards – many thanks for your generosity and your warm-heartedness. Thanks, too, to Veronica du Plessis and her husband Nico, the custodians of the Choet Visser Rugby Museum in Bloemfontein. As the late Choet's daughter, Veronica was my guide through the museum. She also allowed me access to books, programmes and anniversary brochures I would not have been able to find otherwise. Thanks for your time and hospitality both of you. Finally, a big thanks to my good friend and former colleague Clinton van der Berg. Without even knowing it, Clint, you were a fount of great encouragement. You were keen on the project from the very beginning and were always there to egg me on.

Friends, former colleagues and rugby people I happened to bump into along the way who also offered help, time, encouragement and advice include Darryl Accone, Dan Retief, Duane Heath, Donald McRae, John Bishop, Pietman Retief, Albert Heenop, Niels Momberg, Hymie Sybul, Hermann Giliomee, Krish Naidoo, Liam Del Carme and John Dobson. Heartfelt thanks, too, to the documentary filmmaker, Mark Kaplan, for the videos and conversation.

Finally, to the former players and members of the coaching elite. All of you gave generously of your time, but I will always remember my interviews with Johan Claassen, Anton Oberholzer, Paul Bayvel, Hannes Marais and Dugald MacDonald.

LUKE ALFRED
KENSINGTON
JULY 2014

Introduction

THE SOUTH AFRICA of 40 years ago was a country of hearty contradictions. The fist of the local economy punched above its weight in international terms, yet the fingers of that fist held tight the country's riches. Skyscrapers were circled by highways that made them look like the cities of dreams, while lurking just over the horizon were townships with bad water and poor air, where there were few trees and fewer fields on which to play. A paranoid, racially obsessed regime fêted in Washington was in command, yet the old orders of Africa were crumbling. The Portuguese were packing their suitcases, filling Luanda's lift shafts with concrete and scurrying home. Only Ian Smith's Rhodesia (why always that formulation, as though Smith *was* Rhodesia?) stood between South Africa and what we were told was communism's dastardly red tide. The world looked occasionally at the continent's southern tip and wondered – with slight distaste, presumably – what might become of it all. Would the country be washed in rivers of blood? Or would the men in hats allow their power to melt quietly away?

Possibly because rugby developed in conjunction with the rise of Afrikaner nationalism, and possibly because the game was played far away from the centres of the world whose respect white South Africans so desperately craved, the sport had always been tied up with white identity – even, at a push, white soulfulness. So when Willie John McBride's British Lions arrived in the country in the winter of 1974, it was no common tour. They had won splendidly in New Zealand in 1971 and there was a suspicion at large that British rugby was physically and intellectually superior to anything the Springboks might have to offer. Full of loveable anachronisms in tweed jackets, the dominion of local rugby was in an unhealthy phase. It might have been parochial, it might have been decadent, but whatever it was, it was in bad shape. It lacked technique, imagination and international exposure. And that was just the beginning.

It did not help that South Africans were already beginning to feel the pinch of isolation. Before the 1974 Lions arrived, politics had already conspired to lose them a tour to New Zealand and a visit by Wales. Neither were they insensitive to the world's growing disapproval. They wanted to prove themselves by winning but they also wanted to beat the Lions to demonstrate that they were worthy of being played again. It was almost as though they were playing against 30 men.

South Africa had played only one Test since their victorious tour of Australia in 1971, and with a clutch of retirements they were unsure of who their best players were and who was best to lead them. They plumped for '*onse Hannes*', our Hannes, the 33-year-old tighthead prop, Hannes Marais. He would not fail them, the selectors felt sure, but could he do one better? Could he galvanise a team who had never played together before? Could he meld north and south, young and old, English and Afrikaans, the mischief of Morné with the dour workings of Piston in the front row? The public certainly wanted to think so, and they watched it all with a fascination bordering on rapture.

Such was the excitement and public scrutiny that 50 000 people turned up at Ellis Park on a Thursday afternoon to watch the Quaggas, a hastily assembled invitation side, narrowly lose to the Lions. Some weeks later, at the same venue, 75 000 people, almost all of them white, took advantage of 10 000 temporary seats to watch a 13-all draw in a series that had already been decided. It was not long ago, but it somehow seems strangely distant. It was a time before democracy and a time before television, a time before professionalism and a time before irony. In many ways – sporting, political and cultural – it was one of the most exciting and interesting tours of the pre-professional age.

*

When McBride's team touched down at Johannesburg's Jan Smuts Airport in mid-May there was precious little that rugby on the fields of the south could show them. This was McBride's fifth Lions tour and his third to South Africa. His coach, fellow Ballymena and Ulsterman, Syd Millar, had himself toured South Africa as a Lion 12 years before. They had prepared carefully and would prepare with still more rigour at the Strathvaal Rugby Club in Stilfontein before their opening fixture against Western Transvaal. Their preparations centred around the scrum. Well did Millar and McBride know that combat began there. The South Africans were particularly proud of their forwards – it was the seat of their physical and emotional power – and, quite rightly, the Lions decided to confront them where they were strongest. Tactically it was a masterstroke. The Lions thundered across the veld and there was seldom a pack that could stand in their way.

Behind the pack was a Welsh wizard called Gareth Edwards. He was a grand player, deft and quick-witted, with fine hands and marvellous feet, and the gift of the gab when he needed it. Alongside was Phil Bennett, a player as frail as uncooked spaghetti and as nimble as Peter Pan. With Bobby Windsor at hooker, Mervyn Davies at eighthman and Edwards and Bennett the halfbacks, the Lions spine was unmistakably Welsh. Rounding it all off was J.P.R. Williams at fullback. A fine tennis player, a competitive squash player and a handy cricketer, J.P.R. was different. He sometimes wore his socks around his ankles, his hair was longer than the establishment thought it should have been and he sometimes wore a pristine white sweatband. For all this he was a brave, electrifying rugby player. And a dirty one. He frequently ran further than he should have to deck a hulking Springbok forward. South Africans just could not understand him. He was magnificent and brutal; sexy and exotic. Spirited and – with those milky white legs – strangely vulnerable. He was everything that the Springboks were not. He was just like the Lions themselves.

Imagine, if you will, what it was like in 1974. Current South African sports administrators are generally chary of talking about the past, and while there is sometimes good reason for this, the reluctance to have mature discussions about the past in a sport like cricket is nothing short of intellectual fascism. In rugby, the past was a place where, once upon a time, old Springbok jerseys were displayed in the front windows of *platteland* chemists. Folk used to drift into town from their farms after dinner to admire them. They were arranged with care, as one might a museum display case, in little tableaux, with acorns and pine cones and pebbles. And people stood before them and tried to summon words to describe what they had seen and what they felt as a consequence.

Putting aside the folksy sentimentality of such displays, it charms me to think that the green-and-gold jersey once inspired such awe. To some extent we have lost this awe and this reverence for a great game manfully played. And while we have gained many things – the ability to watch the Boks in high definition on television with a craft beer at one's side, for instance – I personally find it impossible to leave behind the idea that we have lost some good things too. We have lost long tours and with them the ability to watch a team meld and develop. We have lost the necessary distance between the giants of sport and the ordinariness of mortals, television thriving on the idea that Bismarck du Plessis is so close that he could be invited home for a cup of tea.

The 1974 Lions were probably the best Lions side to ever visit South Africa. They found Springbok rugby in a rare moment of indecision and vulnerability and, in a manner that now seems almost preordained, they decided to wreak havoc as they moved through the country. This book is about the emotional tremors that have rippled silently and painfully down through the years as a result of it.

Prologue: A dream of all that is good in rugby

IN AUGUST 1962, Springbok centre Mannetjies Roux scored a try against the British Lions that has subsequently been immortalised in South Africa's rugby folklore. While it was an important try – and a barnstorming one – there is no obvious reason to explain why it should have fallen on such fertile ground, why it should have, over the years, inspired songs and sentiment, television programmes and pilgrimages to Roux's home in the Karoo. Is it because it chimed perfectly with a moment of national becoming, in the year after South Africa declared herself a republic, the try representing a symbolic moment of independence through an act of individual sporting brilliance? The Afrikaner historian and rugby lover Hermann Giliomee has spoken of the try's 'zest and ingenuity', and there is a strong echo in Roux's passage of play of the wily Boer pulling a fast one over a traditional foe. Perhaps the try has been remembered so fondly because it somehow seemed to be the culmination of the inevitable. The Springboks *always* beat the Lions, after all; it was as preordained as the frosts of a Highveld winter. While the 1962 series was close – the first

Test was drawn, the second won by the Springboks by only three points, the third by only five – the Springboks still had not lost a series to the Lions since 1896. Yes, the 1955 series had been shared at two Tests all, but the Springboks had won their two Tests well, while the Lions had won theirs narrowly. The Springboks scored 79 points in the series to the Lions' 49, outscoring the Lions by 16 tries to 10. Not until Willie John McBride's 10th Lions toured South Africa in 1974 would the apparent natural harmony of the relationship between the Springboks and Lions be broken.

Looking back at footage of Roux's try, it is, in fact, a remarkably straightforward first-phase score. The ball is won by the Boks from a lineout on the far side of the field, with the late-afternoon sunlight pouring across the Free State stadium, the turf bleached white by the frosts of winter. It takes some time for the lineout ball to be controlled, but, eventually, the bouncing ball is calmed and it finds its way down the line, the action moving from left to right across the frame. In what might be a predetermined move (it is hard to say), the Springbok centres have drifted together and they attack the Lions centres almost shoulder to shoulder. Suddenly the match is telescoped into a remarkably tight space with Wang Wyness, Roux's inside centre, passing to him shortly before he manages to weasel past his onrushing defender. Having squeezed around the first wave of defence, Roux has open space before him. He deftly rounds the Lions fullback and sprints towards the line to score. The try is surgically precise, canny and, in the context of a tight match, unexpected. Through his enterprise and audacity, 'Mannetjies', the little man, has managed to nutmeg two defenders and score a defining try, his physical brilliance supported – and led – by his mischief. The virtuoso try is a demonstration of mastery over space. A move not only deft but magical. This is why fans watch the game. The analysis of the dark inferno that is the scrum's burdened world is for purists. The technicalities of a player's body position as he hits a ruck are for aficionados. Fans want their team to win and they want to pelt the referee with a naartjie or two. They also want to witness a score too remarkable for words, rugby poetry to enliven the blank verse of their days.

Nearly 12 years later, in another hemisphere and another rugby world, another inspirational and much-viewed try was scored. It was scored by Gareth Edwards, the Welsh scrumhalf, while playing for the Barbarians against the All Blacks at Cardiff Arms Park in late January 1973. The move was started deep in his half by Phil Bennett, who would be Edwards's half-back partner for the Lions tour of South Africa some 18 months later. Bennett gathered the ball after a diagonal kick downfield by All Black winger Bryan Williams, and with cavalier disregard for All Black flank Alistair Scown bearing down on him, he allows the ball to bounce before he jinxes his way past Scown; having sidestepped the flanker, he throws his shoulders right before darting left, going past another All Black defender like a matador shimmying past an onrushing bull. Unwilling to court potential disaster and repeat his off-the-cuff brilliance a third time, Bennett passes outside, the ball finding its way to John Dawes, the wonderful Welsh and Barbarians centre who had been such an inspiration on the Lions' victorious tour of New Zealand in 1971. Dawes slices downfield, the All Blacks unable to put a hand on him, when his run is cut off by a group of cover-defending All Blacks, the move emptying of momentum. Yet it has only temporarily stalled, reigniting when the ball is relayed through the slower forwards as they rumble downfield. Tom David, the Welsh flank, has a hand in the move, and the final pass to Edwards is made by his Welsh number-8 colleague, Derek Quinnell. From about 35 metres out, Edwards receives a one-handed pass from Quinnell as he hares for the line and dives over in the corner fully outstretched. It is a try of such freewheeling fun and improvisatory brilliance that the crowd cheers in both appreciation and disbelief. The television commentator gathers his thoughts: 'If that were taken from the pages of a book, no one would ever have believed it.'

At first glance, there is little the Roux and Edwards tries appear to have in common. But what they do share is the idea of the game being turned inside out, of the sport's latent potential being realised in one dramatic passage of play. Every so often a match or a race or an event will approach the limits of what is ordinarily possible, and even breach those limits.

For example, Roger Bannister's 1954 assault on the impenetrable barrier of the four-minute mile at Iffley Road in Oxford demonstrates that what is often understood as a physical obstacle is, in fact, nothing of the sort. It is more accurate to understand the four-minute barrier for the mile as an intellectual or emotional wall. We can infer this from the fact that once Bannister broke it there was a human-sized hole for others to plunge through, which they happily did.

Once the barrier had been broken it was regularly breached. The second sub-four-minute mile was by the gifted Australian middle-distance runner John Landy, and took place on a fast cinder track in Turku, Finland, only 46 days after Bannister's record. Later that northern-hemisphere summer, in an eagerly awaited race, the two ran against each other – at the 1954 Empire and Commonwealth Games, as it was then called – in Vancouver, Canada. After trailing Landy for the better part of the race, Bannister sneaked in front shortly before the end to beat the Australian home. Both broke the four-minute barrier as the walls surrounding the mile came tumbling down.

On the eve of the Barbarians match against the All Blacks, Carwyn James, the great Welsh coach, romantic and intellectual, reminded McBride that the All Blacks did not respond well to having the ball run back at them. These were still the Corinthian days of high amateurism, and the Barbarians were not officially coached. James was not even supposed to be there. Yet McBride and some of the Baa-Baas managed to sneak the architect of the Lions' series victory over the All Blacks in New Zealand in 1971 into their hotel for a chat, doubtlessly looking for inspiration against a team who had missed the Grand Slam only by virtue of their 10-all draw with Ireland the previous Saturday. 'They have never had to cope with having the ball run back at them,' said James. 'Therefore that is what you should concentrate on in this game.'

Of the Edwards try, McBride has written that it would have been almost impossible for Bennett to start the move from deeper in his half if he had tried. But such was the confidence in the Barbarians (four of them had played for Ireland in the draw against the All Blacks the week before) that they were game for anything, ready to push the envelope. 'When Gareth scored I think I was still in our half, puffing along,' wrote McBride cheerfully. 'The whole match was played at a hundred miles an hour and the good thing was that we got quite a bit of ball to give our backs. That was what Carwyn said – just get the ball and feed your backs. They can do the damage.'

Many factors must coalesce in order for records to fall and tries to be immortalised. There must be a flowering of talent. There must be opposition of sufficient quality. There must be self-belief, first awoken, then directed and hardened. Crucially, there must also be opportunity and a welling of desire. All these factors must come together in a manner that expands the definition of what is possible. First the barriers must be approached, then touched, then broken and passed.

When the Lions came to South Africa early in the winter of 1974, circumstances were ripe for the great river of history to kink in an intriguing and memorable way. McBride and his team were, to coin a word they were unlikely to have used, *gatvol*, tired of their regular beatings on the field and the invariable hospitality overload off of it. They found South African rugby in the doldrums, a complacent empire, riddled with barely repressed insecurities and outdated methods. In the weeks to follow, South African rugby's natural introversion culminated in lockdown, the Boks training in prison ahead of the second Test, at Loftus Versfeld. Retreat from Pretoria would lead to the Battle of Boet Erasmus and a kind of cavalier experimentation from the selectors that was so out of character it could only be a sign of desperation.

As for the Lions, their ruthlessness was thinly disguised. Stepping onto the bus to take them to Stilfontein after they had landed at Jan Smuts on the morning of 7 May, McBride looked down at a South African journalist who was considerably smaller than him and, as he put one large foot onto the first rung of the bus steps, explained affably: 'We're here for one thing and one thing only, lad, and that's to fuck up the Springboks' and left it at that. *The Star*'s Mike Shafto swallowed hard. What, after all, was there to say? McBride's boast might at first have seemed like idle chatter, but as the tour progressed it became increasingly plausible. It took the journalists and the South African public some time to work out that behind the easy purr of his Northern Irish accent and pipe-smoking charm, McBride was as tough as they come. So were his pack.

1

British back-story

THE SLOW FIRE of change nibbled across British rugby on several fronts through the sixties. It involved many players and many coaches, but four men – two Irish and two Welsh – helped more than most to put rugby in Britain on a firmer, more confident footing in relation to their southern-hemisphere rivals.

The first outlier was Ronnie Dawson, an Irish architect by profession, who led the Lions to New Zealand in 1959, acting as de facto coach, such was the shambles within the Lions' coaching staff at the time. Dawson was a powerful front-ranker, the epitome of the gnarled, uncomplaining forward, who was not in the slightest bit concerned about the middle-class sentimentality that seemed to envelop parts of the sport in Britain, particularly in establishment enclaves like England and Scotland. He eschewed liquor, thought carefully about the game and was bothered deeply by the Lions' apparent addiction to under-achievement whenever they ventured on tours south of the equator. Ironically, he himself was associated with this tradition not once but twice: having lost the series to the All Blacks as a player, he led the Lions as coach to South Africa in 1968, losing in the dreaded south once again. Despite the losses, he insisted that the Lions could beat the powerhouses of the south if they discarded their sometimes snotty amateur ways. They had to prepare and plan better, as they had done in 1959 when they were cruelly beaten 18-17 in the first Test in Dunedin and succumbed to a late converted try in the second to lose 8-11 in Wellington.

If Dawson tried to drive mental change, proselytising about the virtues of self-belief, Ray McLoughlin, a fellow front-ranker and Irishman, was more obviously fascinated by technique. As a player on the tour of New Zealand in 1966, McLoughlin noticed that the New Zealanders' ability to ruck over the ball once it had fallen on the ground far outweighed what the Home Nations were doing in this regard. Alarmingly, he also became aware on that tour that the All Black scrum was superior to that of the Lions. Described by the *Guardian* journalist Frank Keating as 'grand and deep-thinking', it was McLoughlin who masterminded the idea of a brutal opposing shove on the opposition's feed, in which the defending hooker does not actually strike for the ball. The Irish pack of the late sixties and early seventies were masters of this technique, and Willie John McBride and players like Ian 'Mighty Mouse' McLauchlan would refine the idea of the non-striking counter-shove on the Lions tour of South Africa, with catastrophic results for the Bok pack.

As a prop, McLoughlin was naturally drawn to technical issues relating to scrummaging. He was also sensitive, like few other contemporaries, to planning and preparation, a sensitivity sharpened on the next Lions tour of New Zealand, in 1971. McBride wrote colourfully in his autobiography about the mayhem in an Irish dressing room in the early 1960s, when he was just starting out as a player. The players were required to provide all their kit but their jerseys, and the shed in the corner of Lansdowne Road would be full of last-minute repairs, tightening of boot studs and screams for fresh laces. An honorary kitman would pull fresh laces from his bag, while forwards rubbed their faces with Vaseline and others howled while banging their heads psychotically against the dressing-room walls. The team talk would consist of a good-natured but vague rehashing of received wisdoms and platitudes. The French, for example, were seen to be flaky and mercurial, and if the Irish could put in a good first 20 minutes against them, then perhaps their natural fractiousness would lead them to implode. McBride clearly remembered such quaint Irish rugby rituals while on tour of South Africa in '74, where he gave some of the game's most powerful and carefully delivered team talks in British Lions history.

McLoughlin would have been similarly dismissive of the disorder and directionlessness of the Irish in the early sixties. For him the accent needed to be on planning, on the forwards knowing what they were going to do next. Would the ball be relayed to the wings? Would the scrumhalf initiate a blindside snipe? McLoughlin insisted on greater structure. He wanted the forwards to be more thoughtful, more involved in the entire game, all qualities that inspired McBride to reflect publicly on whether the outcome of the 1966 tour to New Zealand would have been different had McLoughlin, and not the Scot Mike Campbell-Lamerton, a British Army officer, been captain.

Dawson's realisation that the future lay in discarding amateurism, combined with McLoughlin's sense that technique and planning were the sport's new frontiers, would have chimed with Ray Williams's sense of where rugby in Britain needed to go. Unlike Dawson and McLoughlin, Williams did not attempt to foist his vision on the establishment from without – for he was an appointment from within. In 1967, before any of the other Home Nations' rugby unions had cottoned on, the Welsh Rugby Union (WRU) appointed him as their first full-time coaching development officer. It was his job to oversee the entire Welsh coaching edifice and bring in a degree of coaching uniformity. He masterminded the introduction of the national squad system and, along with fellow coaches Alun Thomas and Cliff Jones, began the quiet revolution in Welsh rugby that culminated in the great sides of the early seventies. The squad system allowed the Welsh players to be available for longer before a Test than had hitherto been the case. It had the added advantage of allowing everyone to know where they stood in the pecking order, which meant that players from the shadow squad could click into place reasonably easily if necessary.

According to Clem Thomas and Geoffrey Nicholson in their book *Welsh Rugby: The Crowning Years 1968–1980*, Williams's appointment was the next best thing to Tom Jones singing an encore of 'Delilah' to a group of Swansea housewives – well, sort of. 'The appointment of Williams in 1967 was the best decision made by the WRU in my lifetime and, in my view, was fundamental to the ensuing success of Welsh rugby. Admittedly, he arrived at a time when the framework and the enthusiasm had already been established, but it was apparent that there was a need for a professional with considerable ability to guide and structure the new coaching conception.'

With a steady supply of young players from the Welsh grammar schools feeding the traditionally proud and competitive clubs, talent was always there (even if occasionally it came from English public schools, J.P.R. Williams hailing from Millfield in Somerset). Ray Williams and his colleagues shaped that talent, bringing a homogeneity and sense of cohesion and purpose to the system. It was a system that needed not only good feeder schools, a competitive club system strengthened by the comparative isolation of the Welsh valleys from one another, and good players. It also relied on a national working life that was relatively unchanging. Rugby men traditionally worked in the coal and anthracite mines or the steel mills, Bobby Windsor, the famous Pontypool front-ranker, being a case in point. Finally, the system needed visionary coaches. In Carwyn James, Llanelli, Welsh and British rugby found such a man.

James is too easily typecast as a hell-or-glory romantic. He was too shrewd for that, too articulate and thoughtful, and too blessed with the ability to bring players round to his views while conveying the impression that they were thinking original thoughts. Like Williams, James was the beneficiary of a collective administrative intelligence that was not always associated with the times, in that he became coach of the Lions in New Zealand in 1971 without having coached Wales. It was a side of immense talent. The party was captained by the great Welsh centre John Dawes, and also contained McLoughlin (until he was pummelled out of the tour in the match against Canterbury), Mike Gibson, McBride on his fourth Lions tour and David Duckham, the tricky, long-limbed England winger. Rounding it all off was the great Barry John at flyhalf.

The tour started in unimpressive fashion, the Lions losing to Queensland in Brisbane on the way across to New Zealand. But, as they were to do in South Africa three years later, they won all the provincial matches prior to the first Test, as well as the opening Test itself. Unlike the '74 tour, though, they lost the second Test heavily. Despite injuries (Gareth Edwards was hurt early) and the grind of wintertime touring in New Zealand, the Lions bounced back in the third, ensuring they could not lose the series. The fourth Test was drawn and the Lions returned victorious to Britain from what many assumed beforehand was a brave but ultimately useless crusade in search of rugby's holy grail.

At the end of October the following year, James coached Llanelli, with J.J. Williams, Phil Bennett, Roy Bergiers and Tom David in their midst, to a famous 9-3 home victory over the All Blacks at Stradey Park, a match that has pride of place in the annals of Welsh rugby history. The game was played on a grey Tuesday in early winter, the town shutting down at lunchtime as folk nestled around televisions or went to pubs if they had not managed to buy a ticket to the game. Bergiers, the Llanelli centre, scored the only try of the match, when an attempted penalty rebounded off the upright into the field of play and he gathered it up before dotting down. As the final whistle blew, the crowd went berserk. He and Delme Thomas, the Llanelli skipper, were hoisted shoulder-high as the crowd flooded the pitch. Through the remainder of the afternoon and the happiness of the evening, the pubs ran predictably dry.

James plotted the win to perfection, emphasising the need to tackle every black jersey that moved, and stressing the need for parity in the lineouts and scrums and the importance of competing with the visitors in the rucks. His dressing-room address before the match was a masterclass in economy. There was no hysteria or excess emotion. Everything was calm and measured.

Sometimes he offered advice, sometimes encouragement. There was seldom a wasted word.

Despite the occasional, much-celebrated defeat, the All Blacks lost only five times on their gruelling 33-match tour, a remarkable statistic for an expedition that started in British Columbia on 19 October 1972 and finished the following year, the Kiwis suffering their final defeat on 10 February 1973 at Parc des Princes, where they went down 6-13 to France. Then again, there is evidence from the results and the stories, anecdotes and histories that something had changed when it came to encounters with the men with the silver fern on their jerseys. The halo of All Black invincibility did not shine with quite the same lustre as it once had. British rugby was finding itself, its range and its identity. No more was there the situation, as described by McBride on the 1966 tour of New Zealand, where tour management was so hopeless that for lack of other available facilities the forwards trained on an airfield near Queenstown on the South Island one morning. Just when they were getting into some kind of rhythm they would be forced to hurry towards a hangar in search of shelter, a light aircraft getting slowly bigger in the distance.

Although it was only France of the five northern-hemisphere unions that managed to beat the All Blacks (the Irish drawing 10-all and the Welsh losing 16-19), the period was notable for a raft of other impressive victories for teams from the British Isles over their illustrious southern rivals. In successive years, for example, John Pullin's England won one-off Tests against New Zealand and South Africa, both of them played away from home. Shortly before Christmas 1973, the Welsh hammered the visiting Australians 24-0 at Cardiff Arms Park, an early indication that they would be no pushovers when it came to the Five Nations Championship the following year. British rugby was in a self-evident epoch of success. Competitions were competitive and clubs were thriving. Boys wanted to be like the young men they watched. It was a gilded age.

At the tournament's conclusion, the 1974 Five Nations Championship table had a slightly congested look about it, with all five teams spread across a two-point swing. The Championship was won by Ireland, with five points from four matches, thanks to two wins, a draw and a loss, although McBride said at the time that the victory was slightly hollow because Ireland did not play in the final weekend of the competition. Scotland were next, with four points, thanks to two wins and two losses, followed by Wales, who pipped France on points difference, who were in turn a point better than England, who finished with the wooden spoon on three points after managing only a single win.

But what a victory it was, a storming 16-12 win over Wales at Twickenham on 16 March 1974 in which Andy Ripley, the Rosslyn Park back-rower, played himself into the Lions touring side to South Africa with a larger-than-life performance. Many observers had expected Wales to march to the title, which they would have done had they beaten England that day. Going into the game, they had four points, having beaten Scotland (6-0) and drawn with France (16-all) and Ireland (9-all). A victory at Twickenham was always going to be awkward, but it seemed far from statistically improbable in the light of previous results. Until the win, England had not beaten Wales in 11 years and, further, had not won against them at Twickenham for 14. As it was, England denied Wales mainly due to 'forward power', according to Thomas and Nicholson. 'Each side scored a goal and two penalties,' they continued, 'but England also got the crucial second try.'

While the England pack dominated, there was a cussed little battle within the war. Both hookers – Pullin for England, Windsor for Wales – were Lions contenders. Despite his experience, Pullin was already at a disadvantage because the British coaching consensus at the time favoured hookers throwing into lineouts, something Windsor was comfortable with but Pullin was known to dislike. Sages such as Carwyn James, Syd Millar and Clive Rowlands, the then Wales coach, favoured the hooker throwing in because, they argued, it left the blindside winger free to pursue either attacking or defensive duties, as the situation demanded. In the end, Windsor outplayed Pullin, so it was he (with Ireland's Ken Kennedy as back-up) who made the final party on the tour of a lifetime. Despite an essential shyness, the tour was to be the making of him.

By the time the 1974 Five Nations was complete, it was simply a matter of rolling the final tour machinery into place. Team members were notified of their selection by letter and the Four Home Unions Committee (FHUC) issued a release to the press. At this stage, Millar, the coach, and Alun Thomas, the manager, had already been appointed for nearly a year by the FHUC under the chairmanship of John Tallent, a former England player of the 1930s and former president of the Rugby Football Union. Tallent was helped by the FHUC secretary, Albert Agar, himself a former player, the two being an important and largely unsung part of an administrative infrastructure that presided over the most successful Lions tour the rugby world has ever seen.

The appointment of Millar and Thomas in mid-July 1973

was sensible. It was they who liaised with a representative from each of the four Home Unions to put names forward and discuss claims and counterclaims. The selectors watched the autumn internationals and the Five Nations, and met and exchanged views. Eventually, a week after the competition's end, the side and captain were announced via a press release from FHUC headquarters. By contemporary standards it was an understated affair. There was no press conference and no live television announcement; there were no bells and whistles or flash interviews; no flagrant punts for sponsors or one-on-ones for select members of the weekend press. For all this, there was still much for the media and public at large to digest. Several likely candidates had by that stage already retired from international rugby or declared themselves unavailable. Duckham, the rangy England wing was in this category, as was his fellow winger, the Welshman Gerald Davies. Dawes, captain of the 1971 Lions to New Zealand, and fellow traveller on that tour, Tom Kiernan, retired before the start of the 1973/4 season, so they were ineligible. Mike Gibson, another of the class of '71, originally also declared himself unavailable but his arm was twisted when Alan Old was injured in the match against the Proteas in the week before the first Test. He flew out as Old's replacement after just having been appointed to the board of Bushmills Distillery, one of the finest producers of whiskey in all of Ireland.

According to British rugby historian John Griffiths, it was not the omissions but the back-row choices that caused the most surprise:

> Syd Millar made no secret of the fact that he wanted to play a forward-oriented game. That meant big forwards for the

> Tests especially on the blind-side (where Quinnell had been such a success in New Zealand in 1971). [The Welshman] Dai Morris was probably too much of a whippet-flanker for South Africa, though the choice of Tony Neary and Stewart McKinney (an Ulsterman like Millar and McBride but not an Ireland regular that season) were seen as surprising, both being of the Morris build. Slattery was a shoo-in, having been a success on the 1971 Lions tour. In the event, it was the lock forward Roger Uttley who became the anchor-man at #6 in the Test back-row. He'd never played in the role for England before but had the build of Quinnell and, as it turned out, was the ideal guy for the blind-side job. I suspect Millar and his co-selectors did a shrewd job picking horses for courses. Pullin and arguably Quinnell were the only really unlucky ones regarding non-selection. It has to be said, moreover, that SA were abysmally weak that year: several other British sides might well have won the series come what may.

All in all, the party of 30 contained a fairly even spread from the four unions: nine Welshmen, eight Englishmen, seven Irish and six Scots. Coach Millar, the Irishman from Ballymena, had a long association with McBride, the banker sometimes from Belfast but usually of Ulster, who would be his captain. Millar had come to South Africa as a Lion on McBride's very first Lions outing in 1962. Rounding it all off was the manager, Thomas, who had toured South Africa as a Lion in 1955 and travelled to the Republic nine years later as assistant coach with the 1964 Welsh. Unlike the two Irishmen, who were forwards, Thomas had been a back, so all bases were covered. Having all played in

South Africa as Lions before, the three had a good idea of what to expect. It was not going to be a soiree with canapés, good Cape wines and a violin quartet in the corner.

*

In his report to the FHUC after the 1971 Lions tour to New Zealand, Carwyn James was of the opinion that the tradition of the party spending a week preparing in Eastbourne on the English south coast before departing was a waste of time. They would be better served, he wrote, by spending time acclimatising in the country they were visiting. The FHUC committee heeded this advice and decided the team would train at Stilfontein, a well-appointed sporting complex in the Western Transvaal owned by the gold mines, arriving a full eight days before their first match against Western Transvaal. First they needed to gather – at the Britannia Hotel in Grosvenor Square in central London – to kit themselves out and stay out of harm's way. A group of Peter Hain's anti-apartheid demonstrators was sniffing for the Lions' hideaway and so the players were forced to keep low profiles and use back entrances when leaving. Eventually the protesters tracked them down and in what now seems like a sad little pre-choreographed ritual, McBride received a petition from Hain and listened politely to his views. He was reluctant to enter into debate, for he had other things on his mind.

McBride gave several important team talks on tour, but none tested his powers of charisma – and none was more theatrical and calculating – than the talk he gave at the Britannia. Once the team had gathered, and Millar and Thomas had spoken, McBride went on to welcome the team as their captain. He acknowledged that the tourists were under great pressure not to tour. If they had any doubts that they were not on the correct path, he said, they should express such doubts now and leave the room. After all, it was no good to him and the team if those doubts expressed themselves while they were in South Africa. The doors were open, McBride said – and they were, he had intentionally kept them so – and any man with qualms should leave now. There will be no stain on your character if that is your decision, he concluded, and no accusations, but you must put your doubts aside and be committed to the cause. 'And not a soul moved,' said McBride. 'I believe that was the moment when the 1974 British Lions united and became a special team. When we went off to South Africa the next day, there was a special bond already among us, quite unlike any I had ever known before on a Lions tour.' What McBride does not mention is that through all of this there was not a murmur. Once the captain had finished his speech, the silence grew and grew, stretching seemingly endlessly. Eventually Windsor could stand it no longer. 'I'm bloody well going to enjoy this,' he shouted in his broad Welsh accent, much to the delight of his new teammates.

It would not be fair to say there were no doubters in the rugby community, although the player with the most frequently expressed misgivings was not in the room at the Britannia Hotel that day. The man who had significant moral and political qualms about touring was the London Welsh forward John Taylor. As a tearaway blindside flanker, Taylor toured South Africa in 1968 aged 22, and was part of the successful team to New Zealand three years later. He was a young man in 1968 and desperately wanted to tour, despite certain reservations. These were widened while on tour because he was injured early on and had more free time than would have usually been the case. He remembered with particular vividness an early altercation with some locals. 'They were pretty uncompromising and very up front about how to treat non-whites, so it was in my face from the start,' he said. 'I also met up with an old school pal who was doing a master's degree and teaching black kids in Joburg in the basement of the Methodist church – it was all illegal and he eventually got kicked out in 1970 after 180 days in detention – and that opened my eyes still further. Because I was injured in my first match and couldn't train for several weeks I had plenty of time to explore the real South Africa, and it was pretty ugly. At that time apartheid was being strengthened by new laws; there was no question of softening the stance.'

Taylor taught at a multiracial South London comprehensive until 1972, an experience which, if anything, helped to refine his loathing of apartheid. Playing his rugby at London Welsh alongside the great John Dawes, Taylor shared a house with Mervyn Davies, the famous Welsh number 8. Naturally they got talking about the next Lions tour. 'I shared a house with Merv until about 1973,' he told me, 'and we talked about it [touring South Africa in '74] quite a bit. I understood that many of the guys didn't feel the same way as I did – perhaps didn't care. All I ever said was "Look, I went and hated what I saw. If you feel the same it would be great if you made that known because it would help enormously, but it's entirely up to you."'

Proclaiming that the brotherhood of man was far more important than any narrow allegiance to a particular sport, Taylor's was no knee-jerk reaction to the iniquities of apartheid. He sensed, for instance, that English-speaking white South

Africans were natural hypocrites because they – in his view – hid behind the more politically bumptious Afrikaners and were happy to do so. Being a close friend of Hain's, he also knew that white South Africa was at its most vulnerable when it came to sport, because sport was integrated into the everyday life of white South Africans like few other places in the world.

'When I went to South Africa [in '68] I soon realised that nothing would change unless we could somehow put pressure on the government through the white population,' said Taylor. 'I came to the conclusion [that] a sporting boycott was a good way of doing this because they were so fanatical about cricket and rugby. My reasoning was that nothing would change unless you hit them with something that really interfered with their way of life, and sport was quintessentially their way of life. I do believe the sporting boycott contributed enormously in bringing about reform. The oft-quoted mantra from the apologists for apartheid in the United Kingdom that sport and politics should not mix always struck me as being the biggest nonsense I have ever heard.'

While Taylor was always sure of the ground on which he stood, the farcical circumstances surrounding his non-appearance in 1974 are worth recounting. Although it was widely known that he was unlikely to tour were he to be chosen, he nevertheless received an invitation to make himself available. This coincided with him being dropped from the Welsh side, the consequence, he maintains, of a 'bit of a dip' in form, although others suggest he was being punished by the WRU. Not making himself available meant he was never considered for selection, so of course he did not tour. It was a decision with which he has remained comfortable through the years, although his politics were not as easily accepted elsewhere in the rugby establishment.

'Mervyn Davies got flu on the Thursday before the game and John Dawes [the Baa-Baas skipper] was asked who should come in,' said Taylor of the famous match against the All Blacks at Cardiff Arms Park in 1973. 'He said: "Well, you've got to bring in J.T., he should have been in the team in any case." At which point Brigadier Glyn Hughes, the Barbarians president, apparently exploded and said, "He's not playing; the man's a communist."'

2

International arrivals

As the SAA *Drakensberg*, with its fondly remembered orange and blue livery, landed at Jan Smuts at 7:30 on the morning of 7 May 1974, Dr Danie Craven and Piet Koornhof, the minister of sport, were waiting for the Lions on the tarmac. Given the uncertainty surrounding the tour and the good-natured doggedness of Hain's demonstrators in London, their slightly strained smiles as the jumbo taxied to a stop suggested that here were two highly relieved men.

The Lions' arrival was the culmination of months of planning. Alex Kellermann, the secretary of the South African Rugby Board (SARB), had been liaising with his provincial counterparts and the FHUC for months. Every internal flight was booked, every hour filled, the matches against the North-Western Cape at Upington and the North-Eastern Cape in Aliwal North having dropped off the itinerary at the last minute. Whether it was a trip to a pineapple-canning factory on a quiet afternoon or an outing to the drive-in, the Lions had a full schedule both on and off the field. In a tour lasting two-and-a-half months they would play 22 matches, including visits to Windhoek and Salisbury to play against South West Africa and Rhodesia respectively. They were scheduled to play four Tests, as well as matches against all of the major provincial sides and midweek fixtures against the Southern Universities and the Quaggas, an Invitation XV. It was a match that was to end badly as the frustrated Ellis Park crowd pelted referee Ian Gourlay with a volley of naartjies before a white-shirted spectator tackled him from behind as he was running for cover after the final whistle.

For the first time ever a visiting Lions side would also play against African and coloured opposition. This was the extension of an experiment that had first been undertaken two years before, when Pullin's England had played the Coloured XV (11-6 to England, Errol Tobias scoring the coloureds' points from two penalties) and the SA African XV (won by England 36-3) within the space of three days. Significantly, the Lions were to play against no racially mixed teams. That would come later, with Morgan Cushe, 'Turkey' Shields and Dusty Noble playing in a largely white side for an SA Invitation XV against the visiting French at Newlands in 1975. For the time being, South African rugby policy mirrored that of the Nationalist government: the different race groups could play against one another – as they were to do in football that month, when whites, blacks, Indians and coloureds played in a quadrangular tournament dubbed the Multi-National Games at the Rand Stadium – but could not actually play together in the same side. Having footballers of different race groups – say a nuggety Portuguese South African defender playing alongside a talented Zulu striker – was an intellectual and emotional bridge too far for contemporary football administrators. Despite pushing and shoving from the sides, this was also rugby's view.

While Koornhof grinned, shook as many hands as possible and mumbled a few quick, inaudible words, Craven decided against idle pleasantries, for the dogs of isolation were barking loudly. The Welsh had cancelled a tour in 1973 and New Zealand's Labour government had also prevailed upon their rugby authorities to sacrifice the Boks' incoming tour that year. Kiwi prime minister Norman Kirk feared that Christchurch's hosting of the 1974 Commonwealth Games would be compromised by boycotts should the Boks play high-profile rugby in New Zealand in the year prior to the Games, so the invitation to the South Africans was revoked. Further back, the 1969/70 Bok tour of Britain had attracted controversy and unpleasantness, and while the tour to Australia a year later had not generated the same degree of opposition, the Springboks encountered massive inconvenience. Peter Cronje, who along with Morné du Plessis was on his first overseas tour, remembered that the luggage-handling union serving Qantas's internal flights was not prepared to transport the Boks' luggage. As a result, the tourists flew across the sun-swept deserts of Australia in a flotilla of light aircraft. 'We'd all arrive at the airport beforehand and have to be weighed,' Cronje recalled. 'They'd see to it that none of the light aircraft and the Cessnas was too heavy, so the forwards mixed with the backs, and then we'd take off in this fleet. I remember crossing the Nullarbor Plain from Perth to Adelaide. We must have stopped to refuel about four times.'

The Springboks had not, in fact, played away from home since that successful tour of Australia in 1971; and they had not played a Test since 1972 – when they lost 9-18 to England at Ellis Park. Their rugby, and the sense they made of the game, was beginning to suffer. They needed the Lions as much as the Lions needed them. 'We are grateful that a team like the British Lions has finally taken a stand against interference in sport and we hope that the rest of the world follows their example,' Craven said in Afrikaans shortly after the Lions touched down. Millar, the visiting coach and a man deeply familiar with what the hosts would offer, had a couple of thoughts of his own. He commented on the 'big psychological breakthrough' in the British game since the successful 1971 tour of New Zealand. 'They set new standards,' said Millar in conclusion. 'I firmly believe we have the talent in this present side to match those standards.'

Despite Craven's solemn tone, the mood in the arrivals lounge was far from glum. Thousands of supporters, mainly expatriates and British contract workers, had come out to greet their countrymen, buses having been specially chartered for the occasion. Each member of the touring party had a carnation fixed to the lapel of his blazer. Gareth Edwards, sporting a thin moustache he was to have second thoughts about as the tour progressed, smiled for the newspaper cameramen. Courtesy of the local citrus exporter Outspan, a giant motorised orange was on hand to add a touch of the surreal, the Outspan girls in their skimpy dresses reminding those present that 'You are now in the land of the Springbok and the golden Outspan orange'. There was no official press conference; the journalists literally had to fight through the waiting throng for a quick interview and a quote. After an hour or two of speeches and happy mayhem, the Lions took James's advice and boarded their luxury bus for eight days of intense altitude training at Stilfontein, leaving Bobby Windsor behind to be taken off to hospital with a case of gastroenteritis. For the rest of the squad it was significantly better than being billeted in genteel Eastbourne.

Choet Visser, the designated liaison man seconded to the

Lions by the SA board, took advantage of the nearly three-hour trip down to Stilfontein by sitting next to McBride. Visser had first acted as local manager when France came to play against the Boks in Bloemfontein in 1971. His role was broadened the following year when he became the fully fledged liaison man for the three-week tour by Pullin's England. By 1974 his duties had been expanded still further: he was to help liaise with locals, entertain, and act as a fixer and factotum, all the while keeping his beloved briefcase close at hand. Part of his brief also included the submission of a report to Kellermann after every match, which included items on 'the spirit in which the game was played' and 'the number of spectators and their behaviour'. Visser had already impressed McBride by the time they sat down because he had got hold of photographs of every Lion in the party beforehand so that he could greet them by name as they passed through Jan Smuts. Some were easy to spot: Alan Old's face was all ears and sharp angles; Fran Cotton had a broad face and a slightly puzzled expression in his eyes; Dick Milliken, the Bangor centre, had a sponge of curly brown hair; Phil Bennett carried his mischief around with him like a dear friend. Visser had clearly done his homework because he could identify the more tricky Lions as well as those who might be mistaken for someone else. He could tell his Tony Neary from his Ken Kennedy, his Tom Grace from his Chris Ralston. It was an impressive display.

McBride's initially positive impressions turned to admiration when Visser confided in him a couple of days into their Stilfontein stay. 'I must get one thing off my chest so that we both understand each other,' McBride remembered Visser telling him. 'I am South African through and through. I will be one hundred per cent supportive in the provincial games, but in the Tests I will absent myself the day before or on the morning of the game. And there is one other thing. I am a born Orange Free Stater. I can't be with you before the Free State game because that would be wrong. And, anyway, they are going to beat you, just you wait and see.'

In later years, Mike Burton, the Gloucester prop, remembered the days in the shady Three Fountains hotel in Stilfontein with great nostalgia. He roomed with his English compatriot Chris Ralston and Welshman Tom David. Their early-morning ritual was unvarying. Ralston's alarm went off at 6:30 on the dot. Turning it off, the flanker would reach for his cigarette lighter on the nearest bedside table, combing his long hair away from his face with a sleepy brush of his hand. Having found his lighter, he would light the first of 20 cigarettes of the day, coughing as he did so. 'At this Tommy David would complain that athletes like us shouldn't be subjected to smoke abuse at any time, let alone before daybreak,' said Burton wistfully.

As their stay at the Three Fountains progressed, the Lions began to assert themselves domestically. They expressed their breakfast likes and dislikes, despite occasionally being *vloeked* in Afrikaans by the hotel's resident parrot, Piet, as they trooped sleepily into the dining hall. They preferred their eggs fried in butter, not oil, they told Freda van Heerden, the hotel manageress, and many of them developed a liking for *boerewors* to go along with their bacon. By the time of this, his third tour to South Africa, McBride was already a biltong connoisseur, enjoying kudu biltong in particular. He did not have many Afrikaans words or phrases in his vocabulary, but if there was ever *padkos* (a word he knew) on offer he was more than happy to partake of food on the road. Andy Ripley, the England loose forward dubbed St Francis of Assisi because of his long hair and his love of animals, occasionally arrived at breakfast barefoot. Andy Irvine, the Scots fullback and winger, did one better, arriving at the breakfast table sans shirt one morning. Alun Thomas took him aside and told him to dress more appropriately.

'Ripley was like a student,' remembered *Volksblad*'s Herman le Roux, 'always reading. He was a bit funny, a bit otherwise. He used to have this little portable radio with him and he was always listening to funny music.' Early on in their stay, Ripley found a blind white cat wandering around the hotel beer garden and happily adopted it. He frequently took a saucer of milk from the meal table to feed it, and one of the running stories in the local press at the time was whether the cat would survive when the Lions had to leave the hotel for their match against South West Africa. There was talk of the cat having to be put down if a home could not be found for it, but after weeks of sentimental concern in the broadsheets, the story had a happy ending. A married couple read of its plight and drove from Pretoria to rescue it – much to Ripley's delight.

As the tourists settled in to life at the Three Fountains, with training in the morning, golf or a quiet trip to the Klerksdorp Game Reserve in the afternoon, and a smorgasbord in the evening, Van Heerden and her husband, Doep, started to breathe more easily. The lawns were immaculate when the Lions arrived and the rooms had all been freshly painted. Van Heerden's friends and colleagues wondered why she had bothered, assuming the Lions would go on the rampage and destroy everything in their path. 'Before they arrived, people asked: "Why are you painting the place, it's going to be in such a state", but I have no complaints,' she told the *Rand Daily Mail*. 'They haven't ripped the place apart.' Instead they took off their shirts (they were forever taking off their shirts in South Africa) and worked on their tans around the pool. Edwards, having made the bold decision to shave his upper lip, was photographed on the putting green of the local golf course. He was all in blue, down to the brushed suede of his blue Adidas sneakers. Windsor bounced into camp after being nursed back to health in a Johannesburg hospital. Early on in the tour it became a habit of his to wake his Scots roommate, Billy Steele, to ask him to please sing 'Flower of Scotland' to him one more time. He did not want to be the only member of the party at sixes and sevens in the next team singalong.

From management's point of view, Stilfontein was hardly a random choice. The two rugby fields at the Strathvaal Rugby Club were well covered with grass, there was a degree of privacy and the rugby could be played at altitude, Stilfontein sitting at approximately the same height on the Highveld as Johannesburg. The opening match against Western Transvaal was no more than a half-hour bus trip away and the venue allowed the Lions to get on with their shuttles, scrumming practice and breathing exercises. The latter were devised by the reserve hooker, Ken Kennedy, a general practitioner back home in Ireland. Essentially they revolved around getting more air into the lungs, and lifting the arms high above the head or at an angle to the shoulders at every opportunity. After having to inhale Ralston's early-morning cigarette smoke, Tom David's day got rapidly worse thanks to the punishing jog-run-sprint shuttles, which left many of the players gasping for air. J.J. Williams memorably quipped that although he struggled with the fitness training like everyone else, he was always given a perverse lift when he turned to see how David was coping, because invariably there would be colourful flecks of breakfast vomit in his beard. While J.J. made much of David's struggles, he was doggedly shadowed by Fergus Slattery, the quick Irish flanker. Whatever Williams did, Slattery was by his side. Nothing he could do shook him off. Finally, the amiable Welsh winger became annoyed. 'You couldn't have an openside wing-flanker beating a Commonwealth Games sprinter in training,' he said. 'It just wasn't bloody well on.'

A couple of days into altitude training – and possibly because the breathing exercises had not had the desired effect – Kennedy analysed the players' blood. He and J.P.R. Williams, a surgeon, did the drawing, but the results were inconclusive. 'A number of our players were quite anaemic,' said J.P.R. 'But they were the players who could run around all day it seemed. On the strength of that, Tony Neary, Johnny Moloney and the other two anaemic players were put on iron tablets and a diet of steaks.'

During the first week of the Lions' visit, Mike Shafto, *The Star*'s rugby writer, tumbled down to Stilfontein with the rest of the press corps. By his own admission he was a little timid, only getting to McBride at Jan Smuts as he was stepping onto the bus, but he needed to introduce himself to the skipper again because he was the ghostwriter for McBride's column in his newspaper. Waiting to greet him for a second time, Shafto watched the Lions train with a slightly jaundiced eye. 'It was similar to what you would do in basic training in the army,' he told me. 'I remember thinking that they were giving themselves airs and graces, but of course there was purpose to what they were doing and that never happened.' Being so close to the action allowed him an intimate view and he was struck at the time by the team's spirited sense of well-being. They were professional, mutually supportive and, crucially, seemed happy. 'That camaraderie of theirs was quite unusual,' recalled Shafto. 'I don't remember any other tour having that, and I covered a fair few of them.'

The perceived happiness was not accidental. McBride had been playing the international game for nearly 15 years and had seen most of what it had to offer. The Lions were nothing if not detailed in their preparation and this extended to never allowing players from the same country to room together (a strategy Clive Lloyd, the West Indian cricket captain, would follow some years later). McBride also insisted on sharing the post-match function duties, with everyone getting an opportunity to speak. Windsor was particularly frightened by this prospect, finding the idea of talking in public absolutely harrowing. Eventually everyone became competent, McBride commenting later that it was a strategy that did wonders for morale. Of course, McBride was also sensitive to the softer shades of leadership. He knew when to lead the team in song (he was a strong, moving singer) and when to extract himself; he was a member of the team but he was also their captain, and he knew instinctively when to remove himself, even if in so doing he courted accusations of being aloof.

*

In the week prior to the Lions' arrival, a Junior Springbok side kicked off their three-match 'internal tour' with an afternoon game against Orange Free State in Bloemfontein. Dubbed the Junior Boks, they were in fact a shadow Springbok side, full of the players most likely to start the first Test, at Newlands, in just over a month's time. A glance at the team sheet (*'Met die komplimente van PJ de Villiers Akademiese Boekhandel'*) shows that the selectors were wrestling with combinations and that several important decisions still needed to be made: there were two names each at flyhalf (Gerald Bosch and Dawie Snyman), scrumhalf (Paul Bayvel and Joggie Viljoen) and openside flank, where Jan Ellis and Morné du Plessis were both being carefully watched. In another clue suggestive of the fact that the Springbok coach and selectors were unsure of their best combination, two names were pencilled in on the team sheet at hooker – André Bestbier and Piston van Wyk.

There was, however, continuity with one important name in this match: Hannes Marais, the tighthead prop and Springbok captain. Marais would remain in this position for the two Junior Springbok matches to follow and the final trial at Newlands on Tuesday 4 June. Indeed, he would captain the Springboks in the first Test, beating off the considerable claims of Morné du Plessis, the rangy young pretender to his captain's throne.

It had been an unexpectedly busy first five months of the year for Marais. In January, former Springbok captain Johan Claassen had slipped quietly into Port Elizabeth, his home town, for a meeting with the rector of the local university, where Marais lectured in zoology. Claassen, now national selector and coach, asked the principal if he would consider offering Marais a mid-year leave of absence, as he wanted him to come out of retirement and captain his country. The answer was 'yes', and so began an arduous return to fitness for the 33-year-old, who had considered his international rugby-playing days a thing of the past. Marais still turned out for Eastern Province, but in a strange twist of fate he lost the Eastern Province captaincy when word leaked out that he was likely to captain his country for one last hurrah against the Lions.

'I'd accepted I wasn't going to play for the Springboks again,' Marais told me one windy Saturday afternoon in June 2013, his dog, Bliksem, dozing on a cushion nearby. 'I captained the side in Australia in '71 and then suffered a detached retina – someone poked a finger in my eye – when England came out in '72 and didn't play against them. I wasn't as fit as I could have been when Claassen came down to speak to my principal, Ernst Marais, so once the decision had been made I started training properly. After work I used to run along Beach Road, four kilometres out, four kilometres back, sprint between two poles, then jog. I had to start slowly because I wasn't in top form. Sometimes I used to pick up those whitewashed rocks you find on the side of the road and carry them along.'

Marais was a Springbok archetype. A man of the veld and of God, he was never happier than when scouring the hills around Stellenbosch for Stone Age implements with his good friend and mentor Danie Craven. After matriculating from Gill College and completing his studies at Stellenbosch University, Marais returned to the land where he was spiritually most comfortable, the austerely beautiful Little Karoo around Somerset East. As a young man he played for the North-Eastern Cape, a side that no longer exists. They played their home games in bustling provincial centres and seats of commerce like Burgersdorp, Graaff-Reinet and Cradock.

Marais had the time of his life in the late sixties, playing his *platteland* rugby hard before returning to his hard-working bakkie on Monday mornings to carry on with his job as an advisor to the Angora Goat Breeders' Association. It was after the Lions' match against Eastern Province, just as he was making his way back into a degree of form, that Marais heard the news that the provincial selectors had decided to give the Eastern Province captaincy to George Barnard. Their decision did not sit well, despite the fact that Marais recognised there was only so much provincial rugby he could play after committing himself to the national cause. 'We were playing Western Transvaal at Boet Erasmus [Stadium] just after I heard the news [of being dropped as captain], and did I take it out on my opposite number,' Marais told me. 'I was just so the *moer* in. He was just a young guy there turning out for Western Transvaal. I just murdered him. Afterwards I just got into the car and buggered off to the farm.'

The Junior Springbok internal tour may not have been the most elegant way to sift talent, but it was a way of saving money. According to Johan Claassen, the SA board was cash-strapped at the time and, rather than having extensive trials with four teams and reserves, it was felt that an internal tour, with matches against Orange Free State, Northern Transvaal and Transvaal crammed into a week relatively early in the season, would help the sifting process. Although the Junior Boks won all three matches – against Free State 28-24, against Northern Transvaal 33-6 and the final game against Transvaal 42-6 – it was moot as to whether the selectors were any the wiser at the end of it all. Three stories, though, are worth telling.

The first relates to Theo 'Sakkie' Sauermann, the so-called 'Sheriff of Lydenburg', who came from nowhere to force his way into the final trial and, on the basis of that, into the Bok front row for the first Test. Rod Hartman of the *Rand Daily Mail* suspected as much when he wrote in his preview ahead of the Junior Springbok match against Transvaal (a game, incidentally, which was watched by several Lions): 'It's going to be the battle of the front rows at Ellis Park this afternoon, of that you can be assured. For when the Junior Springbok team meet Transvaal in the final match of their three-game internal tour, the sparks are going to fly in that workhorse world of those big front-rankers. The A team trio comprises of the Springboks Niek Bezuidenhout, Piston van Wyk and Hannes Marais, while the Transvaal men are the formidable Theo ("Sakkie") Sauermann, veteran Ken Resnick and that human blockhouse, Johan Strauss.'

Two of Sauermann's Diggers and Transvaal colleagues, Peter Cronje and Kevin de Klerk, had very different experiences, the one the polar opposite of the other. Cronje, the Parktown High boy who waltzed into the Diggers first XV as a gifted 19-year-old (Paul Bayvel, his Parktown, Diggers and Transvaal teammate, believes he was his generation's Danie Gerber), started for the Junior Boks at outside centre in the Free State game. By the time of the final trial just over a month later, however, he was nowhere to be seen, having injured himself so badly that he was only considered for the Springboks ahead of the Boet Erasmus Test. He ended up playing with such a heavily strapped shoulder that he could hardly move his lower arm above the perpendicular.

De Klerk locked the Junior Springbok scrum with John Williams against Orange Free State, the Junior Boks winning a close match, having been outscored by four tries to three.

The same combination locked the A-team scrum in the final Bok trial at Newlands just before the team for the first Test was announced, with Morné du Plessis and Jan Ellis the two flankers, and Dugald MacDonald slotting in at eighthman. The Williams and De Klerk combination was at it again four days later in the opening Test, despite Kobus Immelman winning good ball at the front of the lineout for Western Province in their game against the Lions the weekend before the first Test. 'The most salient points of the match were that, in spite of their acknowledged power, the Lions can be tamed at forward,' wrote Shafto hopefully in the late edition of *The Star* on Saturday 1 June. 'The four national selectors who saw the game must be in a terrible quandary over the superb form of lock Immelman at No. 3 in the lineout. Time without number he beat Willie John McBride to the jump, with a display that must have the selectors wondering why they did not include him in their 30 or the reserves for Tuesday's final trial at Newlands.'

It would not be the last time that the Springbok selectors were to scratch their heads and look to the middle-distance for inspiration. The opposing locks to De Klerk and Williams in the final trial were the Northern Transvaal pair of Louis Moolman and Moaner van Heerden, and they certainly had their fans. Claassen, though, was not one of them, and there was a general feeling that Moolman was too callow. The pattern of continuity at lock appeared to have been established by the time the second Test, at Loftus Versfeld, arrived, but both locks were ditched in the sweeping clean that followed the Springboks' record 9-28 defeat. Van Heerden and Free State lock Johan de Bruyn were paired for the third Test, at Boet Erasmus, although when Van Heerden came off in the second half clutching his ribs, it was

De Klerk who trotted on to replace him. Van Heerden's injury was not serious enough to keep him out of the fourth Test, where he partnered with Williams, a sore point, I suspect, for De Klerk. I asked him for an interview on many occasions, but he found himself miraculously busy every time.

*

The political and rugby establishment wheeled out *die groot kanonne* for the Lions' opening match against Western Transvaal at Olen Park in Potchefstroom. Koornhof, apparently unable to stay away from the tourists, was on hand, having written the official welcome in the match programme, and the state president, Jim Fouché, was in the stands in a dark suit and hat, presumably much the same clothes he would have worn to church the following Sunday. Claassen was there too, training his careful and empathetic eye on proceedings as the Lions played their first match on South African soil in six years.

Cooped up in Stilfontein for eight days, slowly coming to terms with the altitude and the second verse of 'Flower of Scotland', the Lions were in a mean mood that Wednesday afternoon in early winter. They bullied their way to nine tries, the first of them coming from Gordon Brown, their rampaging Scottish lock. Brown had nearly missed the trip. He was doing early-morning exercises prior to the tour when he was run over by a man cycling through the park, an anecdote that qualifies as one of the more bizarre in the rich tapestry of Lions legends. It was, bubbled Viv Prince happily in the *Rand Daily Mail* on the morning of the second Test, an accident that 'almost put a spoke in his career'. 'I was doing press-ups in the park in my hometown of Troon, and this early-morning worker cycles right over me,' said Gordon. 'I saw him coming and felt sure he had seen me – there was lots of steam rising from me – but he didn't. He almost fell off his bike.'

Western Transvaal, in their traditional red-and-green jerseys, provided some early resistance – their 13 points, through a goal, a try and a penalty, were all scored in the first half – but, as the match progressed, they were brushed aside, the dominant Lions' pack subduing and eventually flattening them. An indication of the Lions increasing ascendancy was the fact that they scored 37 unanswered second-half points, finally romping home 59-13 winners. 'The roar of the British Lions echoed around the whole country yesterday, as they ran Western Transvaal into the Olen Park turf with a devastating display of attacking rugby,' wrote Neil Cameron in the following day's *Rand Daily Mail*. 'It was a display which not only left the home supporters groggy but must have sent shivers up the spine of Springbok selector and coach, Professor Johan Claassen.'

Claassen, a stoic and naturally phlegmatic man, did not appear to be the shivering type. Better described as thoughtful, he would have been thinking long and hard about what he had seen. Bayvel, who played under Claassen in nine Tests through the mid-seventies, told a story about the professor watching Peter Cronje in a provincial game. After the game, Claassen noted that Cronje seemed to be playing with some discomfort to his hip. When this was put to him, Cronje admitted that yes, his hip was sore, but as no one else had picked up on it, he was surprised the professor had noticed. Claassen's greatest gift was that of perception – in both the emotional and the rugby sense. Very little escaped him, and so he would not have been overly impressed with the scribes' lazy characterisation of the Lions' next game, against South West Africa, as being a 'battle for the loose ball' featuring the 'flame-haired Jan Ellis', if he bothered to read the English press previews at all. The Springbok flank was, as expected, in sublime form, nearly managing to inspire his team to a surprising victory. Although it was only 10-9 to the visitors at halftime, the Lions triumphed again, scoring three tries to South West Africa's two. It was far closer this time, 23-16, but the Lions were just beginning to stomp their way across southern Africa. Part of the reason for the comparative closeness of the score was the fact that the Lions were still struggling with the altitude – and Windhoek was nearly as high as Johannesburg, or so the Lions would have it. Mervyn Davies complained of being breathless in the last minutes of the game. While this might have had something to do with his smoking, it is also possible that the Lions were not completely acclimatised.

*

The political economy of rugby during the period was very different to the voracious beast we find today, ever hungry for new commercial morsels and feasts. There were no sponsorships, no broadcast-rights deals, no issues around endorsements, or obtuse lawyer- and agent-driven debates about players' image rights. It is doubtful that the South African Broadcasting Corporation (SABC) and its various provincial offshoots even paid the SA board for radio-commentary rights. So primitive was the commercial architecture of the game that the board made its money mainly from ticket sales. South Africa was still in the pre-television age in 1974. TV dinners around the test pattern and episodes of *Bonanza* would have to wait another year or two. In order to see rugby you had to buy a ticket to the game, and fans bought tickets in their tens of thousands throughout the tour. It was not uncommon for Test matches to draw massive crowds, and even some of the midweek games (one thinks of the Quaggas match, which drew 50 000) were unusually well attended. Twenty thousand fans watched Southern Universities, a patched-together composite side that would never play together again, on a Tuesday afternoon in wretched weather at Newlands. It is an unheard-of number in the modern context. Fans were clearly hungry for the Lions' muscularity, their cutting-edge approach to a game that had stagnated in South Africa, and their exoticism. Scanning newspaper photographs from the period supports the idea that crowds were impressive. Fans were packed tightly together on precarious wooden stands that seemed to reach into the clouds.

Depending on the size and status of the union, the hosts of Lions matches fell into one of four categories. Regular Test unions, such as Transvaal and Western Province, allowed the SA board to pocket 30 per cent of the gross gate; while secondary Test unions, like Northern Transvaal and Eastern Province, offered the board 25 per cent of the gross. Unions hosting Saturday games that did not fall into one of the previous two categories were entitled to keep 85 per cent of the gross gate; in other words, 15 per cent went to the board. This would have been the case, say, with South West Africa, who played the Lions in the first Saturday match of the tour. Finally, unions hosting midweek matches – as was the case with the Lions' third game, a midweek encounter with Boland in Wellington – had to give only 12.5 per cent of the gross gate to the board. Amounts were not likely to run into millions of rands, but the likes of Boland did not host a touring side every year, so the funds would have been welcome.

We tend to make sense of South Africa's isolation in the narrow sporting sense only, but isolation was also felt in people's pockets. The England tour of '72 was brief and hectic, with the single Test at Ellis Park proving to be a negligible revenue earner. Before that, the last tour of any significance was the All Blacks' 1970 visit. In an age when no money was generated through the sale of broadcast rights, four years without a decent tour is a long time. The South African rugby war chest was unlikely to have been overflowing with emeralds, rubies and gold doubloons, although some of the Tests in 1974 did afford savvy provincial presidents, like Transvaal's Jannie le Roux, the opportunity to cash in. He and his executive were able to add 10 000 temporary seats without compromising Ellis Park's safety, meaning that the stadium's capacity for the fourth Test bounced to 75 000. Interest might have dimmed by then, given that the Boks had already lost the series, but trains came from as far afield as Cape Town, Durban and Port Elizabeth, stopping at Park Station from where punters hopped onto suburban trains to take them to Ellis Park's tiny station. South African Airways put on special flights on the morning of the game, and when the ground was finally wedged tight with fans, the Test became the richest revenue earner in the history of the sport, the crowd paying a then record of R525 000 to see it.

This was the age of amateurism, primped and coiffed in all its pompous glory, so despite figures like these, the players themselves received slightly less. The Lions 'earned' a daily allowance of R1.22 per day, while the Springboks received a comparatively generous daily stipend of R1.50 per day. From a touring team's point of view, money went further overseas. This was because you only had to wander out on the main street or towards the bars and restaurants in your blazer on a Saturday night in order to sample the local generosity. It was a simple fact of touring life that somehow managed to escape Ted Partridge, who, in all his filibustering glory, wrote in the *Sunday Times* before the tour: 'When the Lions reach South Africa next month, they will be given the princely sum of R1.22 a day for out-of-pocket expenses – and this pittance is causing a furore.' Whether it was beer-fuelled trips down the Vaal or fishing in choppy waters off the Port Elizabeth coast, the Lions were treated like royalty in the Republic. They never needed to pay for anything, and their liaison man, Visser, was about to embark upon a cunning plan that would see them depart South Africa far wealthier men than when they had arrived.

3

The Springbok template

AT THE BEGINNING of the 1955 season, Johan, the eldest of three Claassen brothers, was plucked from the relative obscurity of playing for Western Transvaal to tour Rhodesia with the Junior Springboks. He made such an impression on Danie Craven, the tour manager, that almost before he knew it he was locking the Springbok scrum against the 1955 British Lions. Although he made his Test debut comparatively late in his career (he was 25), he showed remarkable consistency over the course of the next seven years, only missing the fourth Test against the incoming 1960 All Blacks, a sequence, all told, of 28 Tests. He finished as he started, with a full house of Tests against the Lions of '62, a side containing Syd Millar and a young Ulsterman called Willie John McBride. Such was his standing upon retirement that Claassen was yanked immediately into the Springbok intellectual fold, becoming a national selector at the tender age of 33. 'I was there with Gerry Brand and Jan Lotz and I didn't say a word,' he explained to me from his home in Potchefstroom one bright June day in 2013. 'I just kept quiet because I knew that it was best to see how they handled the situation. I listened to them and learnt a lot because I wasn't on any provincial committee at that stage, so I think I spent the first year or two saying very little.'

The notion of Claassen bypassing hurdles reserved for lesser men has rich precedents in the history of Springbok rugby. Doc Craven played for the Springboks before playing for Western Province, hurtling straight out of the Maties' first XV into the national team after having been spotted by Oubaas Markötter. Morné du Plessis had progressed – or regressed – from centre to fullback to lock by the time he left Grey College for Stellenbosch University in 1968. Once there, Craven took one look at him and promptly converted him into a loose forward, a position ideally suited to his lanky, lopsided brilliance. Mannetjies Roux was another quicksilver talent with rough edges. His under-19 coach at Stellenbosch, Jannie Krige, recognised his skill but was bothered by his unorthodoxy. Craven, however, counselled patience. When Krige went on holiday and temporarily handed over the under-19 coaching duties to Craven, Roux was slotted into the centre position from where Doc felt he would be most destructive. 'I was on my way to my mother's funeral when I stopped for a while to watch a game between Maties under-19s and Van der Stel in which Mannetjies was playing,' wrote Craven, ever happy to trumpet his role as handmaiden to greatness. 'My, how they clicked, and Mannetjies spearheaded most of those movements. The Maties walloped their opponents that day. With Mannetjies in your side you could take on the world.'

If there is a defining story or myth in the literature of Springbok rugby then it contains many of the above ingredients. The tale varies in detail and time, but essentially begins with a talented boy arriving at a Stellenbosch residence (Wilgenhof, perhaps?) from the *platteland*, his duffel bag or suitcase on one arm and his rugby ball under another. With no name and no pedigree but with a fresh, suntanned face and a heart full of dreams, he must work his way through the ranks, playing *koshuis* rugby until opportunity presents itself. One day, someone falls ill or is accidentally injured and our hero-elect finds himself catapulted into an A team or a first XV, where he is watched by the university's resident rugby sage (a Markötter or a Craven), who recognises immediately his hitherto hidden talents. Greatness is indisputably there, they say, thrilled to the core at seeing the boy for the first time, but they are bothered: there is something missing, something they cannot quite put a finger on. Yes, they exclaim, scratching their chins, he is playing out of position. He must move off the flank and into the front row, or out of the front row and into the centre. It is only then that his talent will develop in the manner it should, and only then that the sage can take the credit for recognising in his wisdom that a small – but vital – change needed to be made for the passage to greatness to be cleared.

The mapping of Stellenbosch and South African rugby has other indicators of continuity and tradition. It is told that occasionally Markötter would ask for Paul Roos at Maties practices, claiming that only Paul could show the players how something should be done correctly. Many years later, Craven, whom Markötter had identified as a special talent at scrumhalf shortly after Craven had arrived at the university, moved into Oubaas's house with his dog Bliksem. The dog attended Craven's second wedding as, one presumes, a sort of guest of honour. Craven and Hannes Marais became close friends while the latter was studying at Stellenbosch. Marais eventually named his own dog in honour of Craven's in an act of homage. It was not only dogs. Craven had such a sentimental streak when it came to animals in general that on tour or away at International Rugby

Board (IRB) meetings he would go walkabout in search of them. Those closest to him would only need to locate the nearest pet shop to find him, where he would be talking to the budgies or staring with soft eyes into the fish tank. He loved feeding all kinds of birds, including crows, and would talk to them quietly. As an undergraduate at Stellenbosch he once took a squirrel back to Lindley on the train because he believed the folk of the veld did not know what squirrels looked like and they should be introduced.

If Marais was a Springbok archetype, Claassen was the expression of something even more fundamental, the original second-row forward perhaps, striding meaningfully out of the dawn of Springbok history. This effect is accentuated by some of the oldest surviving photographs of him that show a young, exhausted lock with an almost laughably flimsy scrum cap on his head. By modern standards it looks thin and without padding, more a sentimental than a practical object. Yet clearly it protected Claassen's ears enough to be worth wearing. 'Scrum caps are like cars, there are always changes and new innovations,' he told me with just the hint of a chuckle, 'and mine offered enough protection to my ears. The thing with scrum caps is technique. If your technique is good then you won't damage you ears when you get down between the hooker and the prop.' Of course, scrum caps denoted something more. They suggested – however subtly – that here was a head worth protecting. Those who did not value their brains, the donkeys and the dray horses of the scrum, had no need for scrum caps. Claassen, though, locked with the power of his body *and* the power of his brain. It made sense. He was to become a key figure in the Bok brains trust, after all.

The idea of Claassen looming like a colossus out of the game's pre-history in this country is reinforced by the story of his youth, yet another example of the almost fable-like quality of many Bok beginnings. He grew up outside of Prince Albert in the Karoo. His father owned a rich spread of ostrich farms, some in the Prince Albert and Klaarwater district, others in the Klaarwater and Beaufort West district. The ostrich feathers were almost exclusively for export, and through the 1920s times were good, the ostrich feather being *de la mode* for the fashion-conscious European and British woman of the day. 'In 1928 the bottom fell out of the ostrich market and my father was liquidated – you were getting 10 pounds per bird if you were lucky,' Claassen told me. 'He left the district and bought land on the banks of the Vaal River, where he farmed lucerne. The lucerne was watered by the river.' The Claassen brothers went to school in the area, Johan matriculating from Christiana High in the Western Transvaal before pushing onwards to the University of Potchefstroom for two degrees and, for a period in the mid-1960s, a stint in the South African military. All three brothers played rugby for the province – a dynasty of locks from the banks of the Vaal.

With his high, enlightened forehead and appraising eyes, Claassen told me that God had bestowed upon him the gift of tranquillity. Anecdotes from the time instead tell of a stern Boer patriarch, someone who was obeyed and seldom engaged with. He was, in Dugald MacDonald's memorable translation from the Italian, 'a man of one piece', a man, in other words, of consistent values and ideals, someone who did not waver. With Claassen you at least had the advantage of knowing where you stood, but you never stood eye to eye in a dialogue of equals; you stood beneath him or off to the side, while he occupied an unchanging position in the great Springbok hierarchy in which he was, of necessity and tradition, above you. It was a model that came under severe strain as the winter of 1974 unfolded, and contrasted badly with the comparative sophistication and inclusivity of McBride and the lessons he had learnt from British rugby intellectuals like Carwyn James and Ray McLoughlin.

For all his conformism and Calvinist rigour, Claassen undoubtedly had the gift of insight. Besides being deeply perceptive, he was an unusually sensitive man with a fine memory and a subtle sense of humour. Bayvel remembered a lazy afternoon in Pretoria a day or two ahead of the second Test, at Loftus Versfeld. He was rooming at the time with Gerald Bosch, his Transvaal halfback partner, and both he and Bosch were smoking. They were making their debuts in the second Test and although they knew they should not be smoking, it was a quiet afternoon and they lit up a fag to while away the emptiness that hangs around players before a Test. As they were puffing away, they heard a knock on the door.

Bayvel answered and in wandered Claassen. They chatted, Claassen clearly doing the rounds to check on pre-Test nerves, hoping to offer some calming wisdom, to reassure the debutants if reassurance was needed. Bosch was not able to stub out his cigarette in time, so he hid it under the bedcovers. Claassen was completely aware of this, of course, but the conversation continued politely and eventually meandered towards a natural end. 'We used to sit in the back of the bus with the windows open and have a go at the cigarettes,' Bayvel told me. 'Quite a lot of guys at the time smoked. Anyway, we're there in France and I've just played my last Test. It's the post-match function and I walk over to my table and there, at my seat, is this big carton of cigarettes. It could only have been from one person, and that's Claassen. As far as I was concerned he was brilliant for me. As a motivator, Moaner [van Heerden] hated him. Claassen knew that there was only one way to treat Moaner and that was to whip him to make him crazy. Prof knew how to tap your number, that was for sure.'

With Western Transvaal, South West Africa and Boland safely out of the way, the Lions flew from Cape Town to Port Elizabeth for their fourth match of the tour, against Eastern Province. With or without Marais, Eastern Province players had a deserved reputation for being the thugs of the domestic game, and the Lions were expecting to become acquainted with some of 'the rough stuff', as McBride dubbed it. The skipper had heard from the press corps that some of the Eastern Province players were boasting about foul play and intimidation. He was not about to sit back and wait for it to happen as he might have done earlier in his career. Instead, he called his team together on the eve of the match, explaining that they were likely to be given a going over. If this were to happen, he advised the players to hit whomever was nearest as hard as they could, irrespective of whether they were guilty of foul play or not. McBride's thinking on this matter is worth repeating. In his autobiography he acknowledged that it was an unusual step, but the first Test was only two weeks away. Although he was not playing against Eastern Province, and usually would have allowed the match captain to conduct the practices and team talks himself, McBride said he undertook the step of talking to the team because he could not afford injuries before the

Newlands Test. He did not want history to repeat itself, with provincial teams 'softening' up the Lions before the Tests. It transpired that this was not the only intervention McBride would make in the Windy City. When the match was over he would find inspiration in the settler city itself and add another rousing speech to his growing list of inspirational team talks.

If it is remembered at all, Saturday 25 May 1974 is not recorded with any great fondness by South African rugby followers. The Lions' fourth game on tour lived up perfectly to its advance billing, as predictions that it would degenerate into a running brawl proved correct. Up on the Highveld on the same afternoon, Eastern Transvaal hosted French visitors, Tarbais, in a match that became so out of hand it had to be halted prematurely. 'This friendly will only be remembered for the ferocious fighting that caused its abandonment,' wrote Hartman in Monday's *Rand Daily Mail*, offering the culturally helpful opinion later in his summary that 'the standard of play from both teams was at times as bad as cheap French wine'. It was no laughing matter down south, either, where the Lions were getting closer to deciding on their Test XV. McBride and J.P.R. Williams were both rested for the Eastern Province match, but with the possible exception of the centre pairing (Roy Bergiers and Coventry's Geoff Evans), one of the props (Mike Burton made his first appearance on the tour at tighthead) and Stewart McKinney on the flank, this Lions team was as close to their first-Test starting XV as it was possible to get. Gareth Edwards, captain for the day, was paired with Phil Bennett at flyhalf; Ian McLauchlan and Bobby Windsor supported Burton in the front row; and the pack also contained Gordon Brown, Fergus Slattery and Mervyn Davies at the back of the scrum. In what seemed to be part of an evolving experiment, Roger Uttley partnered Brown in the second row. By the time of the first Test, two weekends later, he had migrated to the flank and a position in the starting XV, as McBride claimed his position back alongside the bonny Brown.

It is difficult to say with absolute certainty but the Eastern Province match appears to go pear-shaped when George Barnard, the Eastern Province number 8, tramples over a prostate Lion early in the second half. Barnard's spitefulness is not picked up by referee Fonnie van der Vyver, but some Lions stragglers witness the incident and punches are thrown as five or six players find themselves in a scuffle while the ball (and camera) moves off elsewhere. Barnard is joined by his loose-forward teammate Kerrie van Eyk, who appears to approach the melee more out of curiosity and misplaced loyalty than anything else; just as he is about to reach the clutch of players, Slattery, rushing towards the action, punches him with a blindside blow of such ferocity that Van Eyk is floored. The match has been marginal up until this point, several players hanging over the offside line, and many years later you can still feel the niggling animosity rising off the screen. Quite why is difficult to say. Maybe the Eastern Province players, comparatively isolated in the geography of the national game, felt honour bound to defend their reputations as provincial hard men? Maybe the Lions were so primed for violence, particularly with the first Test being so close, that they overcompensated? Whatever the whys and wherefores, the match was a mean, poisonous affair, the Lions building on a healthy 16-4 halftime lead to run out 28-14 winners. The try count was shared – three apiece – with the significant difference being made by Bennett. He kicked

16 points from four penalties and two conversions, giving the Lions the cushion they needed, despite a drastically improved second-half showing from the home side.

'Naturally the players were largely to blame for not exercising greater self-control, but the referee, Mr F van der Vyver, too, was at fault for not being firm on obstruction, holding the ball and off-sides play which developed around the rucks and mauls,' wrote the correspondent from the South African Press Association (SAPA) in the following Monday's *Daily Dispatch*. 'The Eastern Province players appeared to be the main offenders in the early stages, playing the man, not the ball, in their efforts to rattle the Lions.' Neil Cameron, in that day's *Rand Daily Mail*, reached much the same conclusion: 'For the most part it was a mauling, brawling, spoiling contest and although it takes two to make an argument, the major share of the blame must be laid at Eastern Province's door.' If anything, Choet Visser was even more scathing, saying in his post-match notes to the SA board: '*Skeidsregter het nie goeie beheer oor wedstryd gehad nie. Vanaf begin moes hy strenger opgetree het. Voorvalle op veld was baie onaangenaam.*' (The referee did not have good control of the match. He needed to impose himself from the beginning. The incidents on the field of play were frequently unpleasant.)

The fisticuffs were not confined to the quaint Boet Erasmus Stadium, with the broad Valiants and Ford Chevelles parked on the sandy rise behind the posts on the ground's western side. After the match, the *Daily Mail*'s Terry O'Connor came out swinging, laying into Eastern Province and their contingent of Afrikaans players with the same kind of abandon with which Brown and Barnard had squared up earlier. O'Connor, initially not sure what this all reminded him of, finally reached for what was eluding him and, with his rhetorical haymaker, described the match as rugby's equivalent of the Boer War. It was a description that incensed Craven and, later, Claassen, who referred to it obliquely in our interview by saying that comparisons of the series to the Boer War were 'bullshit', the one and only time in a two-hour interview in which he swore. The comparison hit Craven hard, for he was of English stock. His father, who farmed in the then eastern Orange Free State, came from Yorkshire and Doc had a strong sentimental attachment to all things English, even British. He was so outraged, in fact, that he felt compelled to address the issue, having taken particular umbrage at O'Connor's claim that 'the Afrikaners' hate for the British' became apparent during the match. Before the official midweek reception for the tourists in Cape Town prior to the opening Test, Craven slyly leaked a story to Hartman for publication in that morning's *Rand Daily Mail*: 'Not only has he upset Dr. Craven, but he has also created some discontent among the British members of the International Rugby Board who are in Cape Town to see the international. For this reason, the SARB president is expected to "put matters straight" when he addresses the touring party at Newlands this evening. One doubts whether he will mention the volatile Mr. O'Connor by name, though he was apparently the only touring British pressman who turned the Port Elizabeth match into another "Boer War", but the chances are that he will speak out strongly against this sort of journalism.'

With the post-match bragging rights indisputably theirs, the Lions were in top form after the game, while Eastern Province dispersed to lick their wounds. The victors broke into spontaneous song at the dinner table at the Marine Parade Hotel that night, a display of camaraderie some of the newspapermen witnessed and found chilling. Shafto remembered McBride taking the side for a walk to the campanile at the entrance to the harbour the following morning, the bell tower erected in 1923 to commemorate the landing of the 1820 Settlers. After that they strolled up the hill to the pyramid erected by Port Elizabeth's first governor, Sir Rufane Donkin, in honour of his wife, Elizabeth. She had died in India in 1818 shortly before the couple were due to arrive in the Cape Colony, and later Sir Rufane commemorated her by changing Algoa Bay's name to Port Elizabeth. McBride was highly conscious of the historical back-story. He knew where the 1820 Settlers had come from and recognised that their narrative would be an illustrative one for his pride. Knowing that the players were feeling good about themselves, he gathered them round. They had been in South Africa for nearly three weeks and all they had planned so assiduously for had come to pass. 'Like the 1820 Settlers,' he told them, 'we now venture into the interior and across the veld. We've played four matches and won all four. The tour begins here. The work begins here – as it did for those brave settlers 150 years ago.'

McBride's grasp of local geography may have been slightly suspect, because there was no venturing into the dark interior after Port Elizabeth – at least not immediately – as the Lions spent nearly three weeks in the Western and Southern Cape. Instead of McBride's inland voyage, the Lions flew to Oudtshoorn, from where they were bussed to an ostrich farm and the Cango Caves for some sightseeing and old-fashioned Karoo hospitality in Claassen country. Two days later, at the Van

Riebeeck Ground in Mossel Bay, they smashed South Western Districts 97-0, scoring 16 tries, six of them to J.J. Williams, three to Geoff Evans and an overall haul of 37 points to Alan Old, the flyhalf. Keeping his habit of playing in the odd-numbered matches (like the first against Western Transvaal and the third against Boland), McBride resumed the captain's duties after the brawls of Boet Erasmus; Bennett and Edwards were rested, as were Ian McGeechan, Billy Steele, Brown, Uttley and McLauchlan. It made no discernible difference one way or the other, the Lions confirming the growing theme of being strong finishers as they scored 60 second-half points in 33 minutes.

4

The Cape of Good Hope

WITH A NICE head of steam, the Lions flew across the great fold mountains of the Western Cape, arriving in Cape Town late in the afternoon of Thursday 30 May. Despite the fact that they had already laid down markers, all but those particularly attuned to their special talents expected them to receive their comeuppance at Newlands. With five wins on the reel, and against mediocre provincial opposition at that, the great chain of rugby being was only temporarily misaligned, argued the naysayers. Things would be returned to their natural order by either Western Province or the Springboks, of that everyone felt sure. In fact, there was a possibility that the Lions might lose both matches. The Springboks seldom, if ever, lost in South Africa, and Western Province had some exciting young backs and some rangy loose forwards. They had only just lost the 1973 Currie Cup semi-final to Orange Free State. Sooner or later the Lions were going to slip up. It seemed appropriate that they would do it in the Cape, the heart of the South African rugby beast.

Despite not being Currie Cup champions in 1973 (that honour fell to Northern Transvaal, who beat Orange Free State 30-22 in the final), Western Province rugby was well organised and competitive. This was partly because rugby at the universities was strong (when Maties were not entertaining thoughts of secession from Western Province rugby) and partly because the club and school systems in both English and Afrikaans high schools were healthy. Seven Province players were picked for the Springboks a week later, this largely because of the optimism engendered by their 8-17 defeat to the tourists. The spoils were shared at two tries apiece and had Dawie Snyman, the Province place-kicker, not missed five penalties, it was argued, Western Province might even have run out narrow winners. In running the ball at the Lions, the journalists believed, Province had found a means to be competitive. This strategy, they advised, should be developed further by the Springboks the following week. Running will be doubly effective, ran the logic, because Phil Bennett cannot tackle and they have no idea of their ideal centre pairing. Whoever they are, there will be gaps for the Bok centres to force their way through.

Neil Cameron's report in Monday's *Rand Daily Mail* after the Western Province game is representative of this argument as a whole. 'In the Lions' previous games there have been hints that they have been a little tackle-shy but they have got away with it, basically because the opposition had been reluctant to run the ball at the visitors and also because the Lions have controlled possession,' he wrote. 'What a different side they looked when Morne du Plessis' gallant and spirited team threw out the challenge, running and attacking from every quarter – even from behind their own goal line. The nuggety little Roy McCallum, Dawie Snyman and the centres Peter Whipp and Johan Oosthuizen carved gaps through the middle of the field as big as Table Mountain.'

Nearly 40 years later it is amazing to consider just how wilful were the scribes' delusions. Indeed, Western Province competed at the front of the lineout and they were brave and thrusting in the centre. Yet it was the brutal magnificence of the Lions scrum that pulsed through the match like a strong ripple in a stagnant pool, rendering all other analysis secondary. Somehow the journalists and South African rugby folk failed to see it; or if they did, they failed to register the import of what they had seen. Perhaps it was as simple as forgetfulness, because the defining moment of the match happened early, in the very first scrum, and by the time Western Province had scrapped and counter-attacked their way to the final whistle, it must have seemed a long time ago. It all happened roundabout the halfway line, in the shadow of the main grandstand, as Roy McCallum, the Province scrumhalf, fed the ball in. Before the Province hooker could strike, he and his front row – made up of two inexperienced university students in Doug Claxton and Roger Bryant – were shunted mercilessly backwards, their balance utterly compromised. The effect is one of two tectonic plates intersecting at a geological fault line. The more powerful plate rubs and pushes the less stable plate backwards, buckling it. What we have, in a manner of speaking, is a rugby earthquake.

After Bobby Windsor's canny hook against the head, the ball came back on the Lions side. Andy Ripley, the second-choice number 8, whose talents Carwyn James had warned Mervyn Davies about at the official send-off dinner in London on the eve of the tour, shovelled the ball to Gareth Edwards, who threw a ropey, off-balance pass towards Bennett, who was sensibly standing in a pocket as far from the scrum as possible. Unable to do much else because of the attention of a Province loose forward, he hoisted the ball skywards, the Garryowen dropping nastily onto Jannie Brink, the Province fullback. Brink was scragged by Roy Bergiers, among others, as the Province forwards wound around him in protection, trying to gather and regroup, while the ball miraculously found its way to Johan Oosthuizen, who, at the time, was being talked about as a possible Springbok centre for the first Test. Under considerable pressure, Oosthuizen attempted a panicky diagonal clearance, but, unfortunately, the ball sliced off his boot and fell not into touch over the grandstand touchline but neatly into the hands of the Lions centre, Clive Rees. He had only to catch the ball cleanly before running the 10 or so metres to bundle over the line.

In many newspapers in the days to follow, there appeared a remarkable photograph. It shows Ripley bearing down on Roy McCallum as the two contest the ball. By contemporary standards it looks poorly photoshopped, as though Ripley's image has been cut out from elsewhere, deep-etched and then superimposed onto a photograph of McCallum. This is because Ripley is so much bigger than McCallum, a veritable Gulliver among the miniature folk of Lilliput. It looks very much as though the two of them should not be in the same frame and, intentionally or not, the photograph stands in ironic opposition to the growing consensus of optimism that, despite losing, Western Province had found the keys to unlock the Lions' secrets. The photograph's subliminal message was that the contest between the Lions and Western Province had been one of giants against men. The rugby public and scribes would have done well to heed what had really gone on in the Lions' sixth match of the tour.

The rugby earthquake witnessed by the Newlands crowd

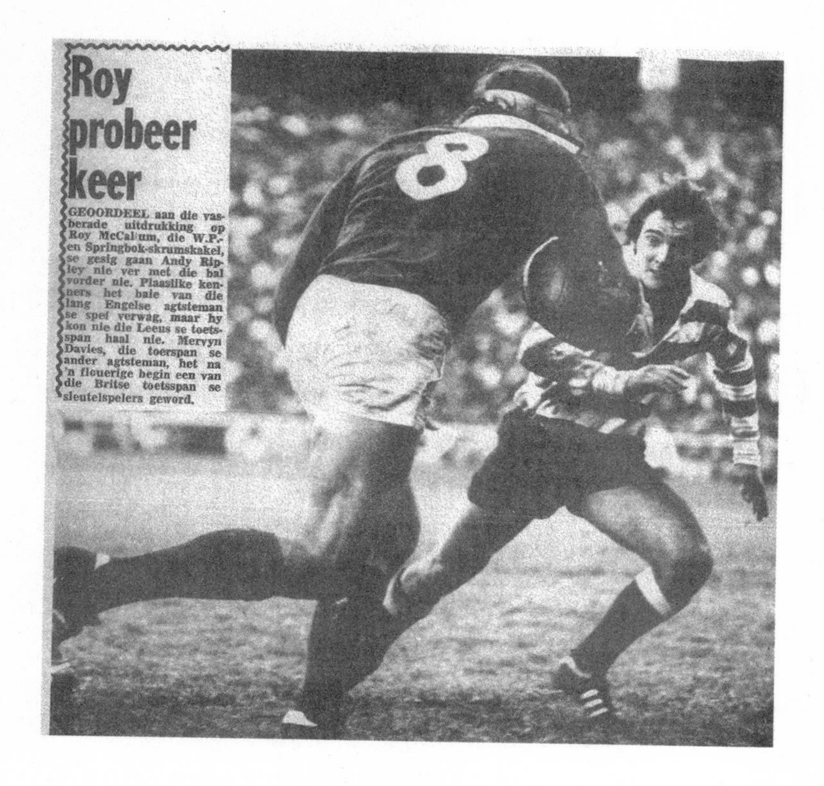

Roy probeer keer

GEOORDEEL aan die vasberade uitdrukking op Roy McCallum, die W.P.- en Springbok-skrumskakel, se gesig gaan Andy Ripley nie ver met die bal vorder nie. Plaaslike kenners het baie van die lang Engelse agtsteman se spel verwag, maar hy kon nie die Leeus se toetsspan haal nie. Mervyn Davies, die toerspan se ander agtsteman, het na 'n flouerige begin een van die Britse toetsspan se sleutelspelers geword.

that day was not serendipitous. Front-row play among the Home Nations at the time was of an incredibly high standard. Not only was power paramount, but technique was vital. In a telling interview in a BBC television documentary called *Glorious Victorious* several years after the tour, Mike Burton was asked about the Eastern Province match and whether Ian McLauchlan got the better of Marais (it was their first game against each other since Marais had scrummed for the Springboks against Scotland's McLauchlan in 1970). Burton's reply was deliberately vague, but after a revealing second or two, a slightly less diplomatic answer leaked out. 'In actual fact,' said Burton, laughing gently, 'the best front row the first-choice Lions packed against was probably myself, Sandy [Carmichael] and Ken Kennedy, the guys they scrummed against in practice.'

After the tours of New Zealand in 1971 and South Africa three years later, McLauchlan was significantly less complimentary. '[When I toured] I was amazed at the generally low standard of scrummaging there,' he growled. 'They were not prepared to scrum low, and the tightheads tried to keep you up rather than making you come down. In Britain and Ireland many tightheads bear down pretty heavily. In the southern hemisphere they stand up, just as they do in Rugby League, where the scrum is simply a means of getting the game re-started rather than an integral part of play.' McLauchlan, McBride and Syd Millar all knew that mastery of the scrum situation was the platform upon which the Lions' success was to be built. Such mastery extended beyond their own feed, for throughout the tour they endeavoured to make the opposition's ball as compromised and difficult as possible. Windsor has attracted the plaudits and interest, partly because he was a Welsh working-class stereotype, but the man in the proverbial scrum cap was McLauchlan. Marais always maintained that 'Mighty Mouse' was the thinker behind the grunt, going so far as to say that on the field of play the pack took its direction from him, not McBride. 'McLauchlan seemed to be their pack leader on the field,' wrote Marais afterwards. 'I know that McBride was captain, but on the field it was "Mighty Mouse" who did all the talking. I only really heard McBride giving orders in the final Test, when things began to go wrong for his team. He got agitated – too agitated, I thought – and some hard words were barked at his men.'

Three days after the Western Province match, on Tuesday 4 June, McLauchlan, with notebook in hand, returned to Newlands with Scottish teammate Ian McGeechan to watch the final Springbok trial. Given what he said in later years about the technical insufficiencies of southern-hemisphere front rows, it is unlikely he would have seen anything to bother him unduly. As it happened, the A-team front row for the trials (in white jerseys) was the front row for Saturday's first Test, with Piston van Wyk at hooker, flanked by Sakkie Sauermann at loosehead and Marais at tighthead. The A-team locks were Kevin de Klerk and John Williams, with Jan Ellis and Morné du Plessis on the flanks, and Dugald MacDonald the anchor at eighthman. Pretty much the same pack would run out for the Test in five days' time, with one notable change: MacDonald was relegated, Du Plessis took his position at the back of the scrum, and Jan 'Boland' Coetzee was elevated from the B team and slotted into Du Plessis' vacancy on the flank.

There was significantly more to consider behind the Bok scrum. On the evidence of the trials it seemed that the five Springbok selectors were in a quandary about who to play at scrumhalf and on the wings. Neither scrumhalf triallist – Bayvel for the A team and Northern Transvaal's Dirk de Vos, who was already a Springbok, for the B – was chosen for the first Test, the selectors plumping for Roy McCallum after his fine showing for Western Province. There was logic to the choice, because Roy was Dawie Snyman's halfback partner at provincial level and the two had a long association. By the same token, was it prudent to draft a player who was unable to find a place in either of the teams for the final trials straight into the first Test? Despite deliberating for nearly five hours, and only announcing their side close to midnight that Tuesday night, the Springbok selectors clearly thought the scrumhalf experiment was one worth trying. As the series progressed, these experiments would only increase in bravado, desperation and off-the-wall creativity. Bayvel was united with Gerald Bosch, his Transvaal halfback partner, for the second Test, with Gerrie Sonnekus (who was nowhere to be found that day of the final trials at Newlands), an eighthman, unbelievably finding his way to the scrumhalf position for the third as Jackie Snyman's partner. For the fourth Test, at Ellis Park, the selectors reverted to Bayvel and kept Jackie Snyman where he was at flyhalf. By that stage it probably was not lost on them that the scrumhalf issue was simply an expression of a more pressing problem: that scrum-halves cannot function behind broken packs.

As far as the wings were concerned, Gerrie Germishuys and Leon Vogel represented the A team in the final trial. Clearly the Orange Free State pair did not impress sufficiently, however, because Chris Pope and Gert Muller, the B-team wings on the day, were drafted into the Test side. Muller swapped ends at the break and scored two tries, so the final trial was a success for him, while the cerebral Pope was selected for his Test debut. There were other issues, too, according to the scribes. The key to them all, said Neville Leck in the *Rand Daily Mail* on the morning of the final trial, was Ian McCallum. 'I believe the Bok selectors have learned the lessons of Newlands [in the Western Province match, in other words], that they have seen the danger of Lions fullback, JPR Williams, and the glaring deficiencies of the Lions midfield. I believe they want the balance of Dawie Snyman at flyhalf, that they want to be able to run "good" ball at the Lions, but they will sacrifice everything for a match-winning goal-kicker. Snyman is certainly not one but Ian McCallum is – and proved it in 1970 when he was one of the arch-destroyers of the All Blacks.'

On that same afternoon at the Goodwood Showgrounds, the Proteas, a team made up of players from the coloured South African Rugby Football Federation, played against the Lions in an ill-tempered affair reminiscent of the match against Eastern Province. The comparison is only partially accurate because, while both matches were dirty, there was something malicious in Eastern Province's approach. The Proteas, by contrast, could almost be forgiven. Watching replays of the Lions' 37-6 win suggests that the Proteas' over-exuberance was partly the result of nerves and partly the result of a growing awareness that they were going to be on the losing side. Matters remained within manageable proportions up until halftime, with the Lions changing round 13-6 to the good. After that it was a case of yet another bullying second half in which the Lions pack turned the screws on the opposition. The Lions ran in four tries after the break as the Proteas became an increasingly ragged and demoralised bunch.

The match is rightly remembered for Christian Cupido's assault on Alan Old, a tackle so late it might have been made at midnight. With the tackle went Old's tour. He was hospitalised and his torn knee ligaments operated upon immediately. In a coincidence not without symbolic significance, driving back to the Arthur's Seat Hotel in Sea Point after watching the final Springbok trial, McLauchlan and McGeechan noticed an ambulance speeding off to hospital. In the back were Old and his flyhalf colleague Bennett, fresh from the Goodwood Showgrounds. McLauchlan recalled in his autobiography that he asked the taxi driver to stop. 'Phil nodded inside and said: "It's Alan; he's had it."' Old returned home shortly afterwards. Never a Lion again, he played his last game for England against France in 1978, and later became a schoolmaster, disappearing into dignified provincial obscurity. By contrast, his two teammates surged forwards into history, their note-taking a sure indication that here were men for the future. McGeechan was to make his name on the '74 tour. He might not have started as first-choice inside centre, but his confidence and stature increased as the tour progressed. Photographs of him in the Boet Erasmus dressing room after the Lions had won the third Test show him looking at McBride with happy relief. There is something like adoration in his eyes.

Once he was settled, Old's hospital room became a sort of railway station for all manner of arriving and departing Lions as he struggled to come to terms with the grim reality of his injury. 'My hospital room became a part-time bar as players, officials and press men did everything they could to help me to get to grips with the situation,' said Old. 'It didn't always work. The first visit by Syd and Willie John was a case in point. Being a stoic Englishman I was quite philosophical, but unfortunately these two big Irishmen were not made of such stuff – they were almost in tears about my bad luck and their quiet voices were laden with emotion. Fortunately I was able to console them.'

Old's injury precipitated the tour's second crisis. Unlike Terry O'Connor's Boer War fandango, this one was never made public, but Visser's daughter, Veronica du Plessis, tells of McBride's insistence that a replacement be found immediately. The chosen man was Mike Gibson, who had toured New Zealand in 1971. Without putting too fine a point on it, McBride wanted him on the next available plane. This put Visser in an invidious position. Normally sanction for a replacement needed to come from the SA board in general and Craven in particular, but McBride was in no mood to jump through bureaucratic hoops. It was only days before the first Test and, although Bennett and Edwards were going to be the halfback combination, Old's injury was a big nuisance. There were the Southern Universities to play immediately after the first Test and Transvaal after that. A week later, after a lightning trip into Rhodesia, was the second Test, at Loftus Versfeld. McBride could not have Bennett, the man with wings on his feet, playing in every game on such a long tour, particularly in the run-up to the second Test. McBride prevailed upon Visser to make the necessary arrangements without authorisation from the board and threatened to call off the tour if he did not get his way. As Visser knew he would, Craven got to hear about the clandestine string-pulling. He was not best pleased.

'Craven summoned my dad to Stellenbosch and asked him if he would like to take his chair because he was behaving as though he wanted to be the president of SA Rugby,' explained Veronica. 'Dad tried to explain that Willie John had insisted that a replacement come out immediately and he was given no alternative. Craven wasn't happy. There was a big fight, *'n groot gemors*. After a while Doc softened a bit. He always used to come down to my parents' holiday home in Hermanus on New Year's Day. It was a great tradition, and it happened again the following year. The agreement was that Craven had to leave Bliksem in the car, he wasn't allowed into the house, so every once in a while Doc went outside to feed him or give him water. So they patched things up afterwards.'

The crowning irony of the crisis is that it took Gibson almost two weeks to reach South Africa anyway, so the Lions had to come up with a plan in the interim. The result was that Bennett played three matches in a week – at flyhalf against South Africa in the first Test, and against Southern Universities and Transvaal – with McGeechan helping out at flyhalf directly after the Transvaal match in the game against Rhodesia. This worked so well that he also played at 10 against the Quaggas and Orange Free State in consecutive matches the following week. Gibson, meanwhile, arrived in Johannesburg in time to see the second Test and, at Ellis Park the following Thursday, he played against the Quaggas at centre alongside Roy Bergiers. He ended up being a busy man, playing in seven of the remaining ten games on tour, although he played at flyhalf in only two of them – against Griqualand West and Eastern Transvaal. Bennett, of course, was injured inadvertently by Ian McCallum at the end of the second Test, gashing his foot and limping from the field. His appearances were rationed after that: he played against the Leopards, mainly to see whether he would be able to play in the third Test; the third Test itself; against Natal; as well as in the fourth Test. Gibson may have taken longer to arrive than McBride would have liked, but in the end he proved to be an extremely useful replacement.

Despite the skulduggery and a desperation tinged with dirtiness, the match against the Lions was a grand day for the coloured rugby federation. There was opposition to the match, with some in the community seeing the players as sell-outs, Uncle Toms who were being co-opted by the whites. Steve Tshwete, who was to become the minister of sport in South Africa's first democratic government, was of the opinion that games like these lent an undeserved credibility to the white rugby authorities. Playing black and coloured teams meant, in effect, having it both ways: internationals could continue as long as racially representative teams could be wheeled out in a controlled and orchestrated fashion. As Tshwete said many years later: 'They [the Lions] should have refused to play against these separate entities. Once they were in South Africa they should have said: "OK we are here, we are going to play against white apartheid sides." And not to give any respectability to elements who were perceived in the townships as being Uncle Toms. We were strongly opposed to international links, but once the Lions were here their victory was important for political reasons because it would boost the fortunes of the democratic movement.'

Hermann Giliomee well remembers having a conversation along similar lines with Craven in Edinburgh in late 1969. The historian was on a six-week research visit to London, spending most of his time in the Public Record Office. As the Springboks were in the United Kingdom at the time, and being a former rugby correspondent for the Stellenbosch student newspaper, Giliomee trundled up to Scotland and cadged a ticket to the Test from Andrew van der Watt, the Springbok wing, who was in his history class at Maties. 'I stopped by at the Springboks' hotel to collect my ticket. While there I called Craven, whom I'd got to know a bit, first as student and later as lecturer in Stellenbosch,' said Giliomee. 'He asked me to come up to his room. He was still in his pyjamas sitting on his bed, and I was offered a chair. I told him that in my view the only way to stop the isolation of our rugby and sports teams was to put an end to the fiction that the Springbok teams represented the entire South African population. Springbok teams could still be chosen from the best white players, but they would no longer represent South Africa. The rugby board had to give a commitment that it would choose black and coloured players the moment the government lifted the ban on integrated sport.

'I could see that Craven was torn. He desperately wanted the Springbok tours to other countries to continue, but he was as desperate to uphold the custom that the Springboks represented South Africa. He pondered my proposal for a while and then said, "No, it is tradition that the Springboks represent South Africa. It would be too painful to give that up."'

As well as the occasion created by the Lions' visit to Goodwood, the fixture was a financial windfall for the coloured federation, with SA Rugby's sliding scale of the profits favouring the smallest or poorest of the provincial unions. A cheque and accompanying letter dated 9 September 1974 in the SARB archives at Stellenbosch University tells part of the financial story. Written by C.L. Adams, the secretary of the South African Rugby Football Federation, the letter states in part: 'Dear Sir – Enclosed herewith find cheque no. 630 874 being for the sum of R2192,15 being 12-and-a-half percent of the gate receipts of the match the Federation versus the Lions. Kindly accept our sincere apologies for the late forwarding of same due to unforeseen difficulties and many thanks for your kind assistance.' Late or not, the bulk of the profits – in excess of R20 000 – would have been kept by the federation, a desperately needed injection of capital. The match was nevertheless politically divisive in the coloured community, driving a wedge between those keen to take advantage of Craven's largesse and those suspicious of his motives, and the motives of entrenched white sport administrators in general. Neither did it cast the Proteas in a glowing rugby light. After the tour the Lions were quoted as saying that they thought the black players of the Leopards (played five weeks later) had a better command of the basics and were generally more skilful than their coloured counterparts. Still, political debates about the morality of collaboration were one thing, fat bank balances with which to continue running programmes were quite another.

The next day, a Wednesday, preparations for the first Test started in earnest. McLauchlan remembered a cold and wintry Cape Town. 'It rained all the time,' he wrote with a clear note of regret. Whether or not this would play into the Lions' hands was a topic of some debate in the bars and on buses. Either way, it did not matter to Claassen; he was anxious to get the Springboks scrumming. The scrum, he felt sure, was where the home side was worryingly vulnerable and where the Lions would attack. The rain proved to be a real impediment, though, and the Boks did not train on the Thursday because of it. The Lions did, taking their bus into the very heart of South African rugby: Stellenbosch. The tour was full of such demonstrations of either mischief or cunning from the tourists. Maybe in this case, though, the decision simply made good common sense.

In another example of Lions cunning, on the day before their opening game against Western Transvaal, the players were allowed to train in Lions jerseys for the first time. This was a transparent attempt to get them thinking as Lions and not as Englishmen, Welshmen or Scots. The purpose was a unifying one, an invitation to become a Lion, a concept that must have seemed slightly abstract up until then. Anton Oberholzer, the Transvaal captain, tells another story of McBride's endless capacity for gamesmanship. Having tossed the coin for choice of ends, Oberholzer led his team out at Ellis Park only to find the Lions already standing in Transvaal's half. Unperturbed, he and his team simply navigated round them as they crossed the halfway line to take up their positions in the other half of the field. Still, it left him guessing, wondering what else McBride had up his sleeve.

Instead of training on the Thursday, the Springboks went in for a spot of *swartbordrugby* – or so it was dubbed in the Afrikaans press. They discussed rules and possible refereeing interpretations in the morning and had what was referred to as 'a symposium' in the afternoon. In the evening the players had a team talk at their hotel. They followed this up by watching a film of the previous Saturday's match at Newlands between Western Province and the Lions. History does not record if there was a shudder of apprehension in the audience when the red machine shunted the Province pack backwards in the first scrum of the match. We do know that Claassen professed to be happy with the day's preparations in Friday's first editions. 'We did very worthwhile work,' he said. 'It was far better than a practice.'

Still, Claassen must have been agitated to get onto the paddock, and, the following day – the day before the Test – the Boks did eventually manage to get into their boots. They scrummed against a strong Police pack at Pollsmoor Prison, and generally the feeling was that the session had been unnecessarily intense. Marais complained afterwards that the scrumming practice was not what was needed at the time, and he – and arguably the rest of the pack – arrived tired at the Test the next day. This seems a trifle ludicrous. Fatigue was a problem during the period, but it was felt particularly by the Western Province players who took part in the final Springbok trial. Some, like the McCallum brothers, played four matches in ten days, playing for Western Province, one of the two teams in the final trial, the Springboks and Southern Universities in the midweek game following the Test. Whether fatigue played a part or not, Marais clearly did not feel the necessary equilibrium. 'I was not as ready for the game as I would have liked to be,' he told me. 'It could have been because we started later that season or that we overtrained. Anyway, we lost to the better side.'

The Lions, meanwhile, were about to witness an unplugged version of *Willie John live at Arthur's Seat*. On the eve of the Test, McBride bid them come into the team room. Everyone filtered in, excited and scared in equal measure. There was a shuffling of chairs, a clearing of throats, the odd smirk and cynical, out-of-earshot jibe. Silence filled the room like water as the Lions waited for their captain to talk. They were expecting words of inspiration, words as straight and direct as the man himself. He had already spoken to them several times. There was the famous open-door address at the Britannia Hotel in Grosvenor Square prior to their departure; his concerned intervention ahead of the Eastern Province match; and, a couple of days later, a piece of masterful extemporisation at the campanile when he seduced them with his 'venture into the interior' speech. What exactly did he have for them this time? Was it going to be inspirational? Simple? Moving? A combination of all three? The Lions waited, wondering what was in store. The silence grew. No one dared speak or crack a joke or look at their watch. And still McBride stood, saying nothing. The significance of the moment prevented them from laughing, from roaring with laughter, in fact. Each, in their own way, at their own speed, realised what McBride was doing. He was allowing the moment to speak for itself. They would not be coming this way again. It was crucial to win the first Test and so establish themselves and set up the rest of the tour. No words were necessary. They knew exactly what they had come to do. They had been speaking about nothing else – directly and indirectly – for the month they had been in South Africa. Eventually the team meeting broke up, the players absolutely convinced that they would prevail over the Boks. For Fran Cotton, who had been rewarded for his excellent form with a first Test cap, the leaden foot of time was all too much. Later that night, he and roommate Roger Uttley beat a temporary escape and plunged through the hotel doors into the cool night air. 'The night before [the first Test] we went for a late-night stroll along the seafront at Green Point,' recalled Uttley. 'It was drizzling but we didn't notice a thing as we went sidestepping around dustbins and dummying lampposts to score great tries in front of bemused seagulls on the seawall.'

From all over South Africa, fans were gravitating to Newlands. Upcountry newspapers showed a photograph of Jannie le Roux, the president of Transvaal rugby, taking a specially chartered Blue Train down to Cape Town alongside benefactor Wilf Isaacs and industrialist Barney Rogoff. 'For Mr. Rogoff, who is 75, it will be the 65th Test at which he has been a spectator,' chirped the caption below three old geezers in fedoras and overcoats standing expectantly in front of a locomotive at Park Station. Not everyone travelled in such luxury. The gates at Newlands opened at 10 a.m. to long queues, with one ingenious spectator erecting himself a swinging seat by suspending a rope from some grandstand scaffolding and tying an empty cold-drink crate to it 'giving him a precarious bird's eye view', wrote Mike Shafto in *The Star*'s city late edition. While the spectators dozed and daydreamt through the curtain-raisers (which all ended 10 minutes early in deference to the condition of the muddy pitch), punters could read the minutiae of the upcoming battle. 'The total weight of the Lions pack is 1726lbs or just over 215lbs per man, with the captain, Willie John McBride, the heaviest at 232lbs and the wild flanker, Fergus Slattery, the lightest at 196lbs,' wrote Shafto. 'The Springboks gross 1729lbs. Kevin de Klerk, the new cap, is the heaviest man on the field at 245lbs.'

De Klerk, one of six new caps for the Boks, and his team spent the morning sipping tea in Kalk Bay, while behind them the demure poetry of the harbour unfolded in regular stanzas. The rain continued to fall. Claassen and Marais thought getting the team out of their hotel would do them good, and discussion in the Kalk Bay hotel revolved around the wind and the weather. As a local, Boland Coetzee was asked for his advice. When it came to the toss a couple of hours later, Marais elected to play with the wind in the first half. It was not a gale, but it was blowing at a considerable clip. The southern goalposts swayed enough for the scribes to mention the fact in their post-mortems.

The Test itself was a spectacle for purists rather than populists. Conditions underfoot were muddy, although some patches of Newlands were more treacherous than others. The forward battle was grim and opportunities for flair and try-scoring limited. Oosthuizen, the Bok centre, handled the ball for the first time in the 20th minute of the second half, the move culminating in him breaking his jaw as he was allegedly punched from behind by a Lions tackler. He played on regardless. Oosthuizen's centre partner, Peter Whipp, handled the ball twice in the entire Test; and running chances for the wings, Muller and Pope, were almost non-existent. Given the lack of running opportunities for either side's backs (with the exception of J.P.R. Williams), the earlier concerns about the limitations of the Lions midfield, with McGeechan and Dick Milliken the centres, did not even come into it. Equally irrelevant was the fact that Bennett was tackle-shy. Partly because they were under *kwaai druk* from Fergus Slattery, the Springbok halfbacks did not have an opportunity to run into the flyhalf channel; neither did their loose forwards, because they had their hands full bailing out their tight five.

Conditions being as they were, both sides played 10-man rugby, reverting to nine when the occasion demanded. Legend has it that McBride knew the Lions had the series won after the very first scrum, and certainly the record of the match confirms that the Boks were timid scrummagers. Gareth Edwards tells the story of referee Max Baise breaking up an early scrum and, as the packs gathered again before engaging, hearing Windsor growl at his opposite number, Piston van Wyk, 'Come here, you pudding face.' Cotton, according to Edwards, 'had to reach out and drag his opponent [Sakkie Sauermann] into the scrum. That reluctance, indeed, diffidence, confirmed to me that we – or at least our front-row union – had scored a most important psychological victory.' The statistics show that the Lions won approximately half-a-dozen more lineouts than the Springboks, despite John Williams, the Bok lock, having a reasonably good game, while there were two hooks-against-the-head apiece. The loose scrums and mauls were shared, with the Lions winning the Test 12-3 thanks to three Bennett penalties and an Edwards drop goal, compared to Dawie Snyman's single drop goal in the first half.

All of this, however, obscures the single most important feature of the match: that the Lions scrum was so dominant that they spoilt the Springbok ball sufficiently for it to be mostly kicked onto J.P.R. Williams, the Lions fullback, or made too difficult to use. This meant, in turn, that the Bok loose forwards were often forced to rally in support of their tight five. They were not allowed the luxury afforded to Slattery, who made an unbelievable nuisance of himself around Snyman at flyhalf and, to a lesser extent, Roy McCallum at number 9. In Jan Ellis and Morné du Plessis the Springboks had two of their finest players, yet their impact on the game was negligible. This was because they were forced to scramble behind a beaten pack, Du Plessis getting in Snyman's and McCallum's way on at least two occasions and Ellis memorably being tackled by Mervyn Davies in one of the biggest hits of the Test. The converse of this was that the Lions earned better ball and, as a result, they were able to control the rhythm of the game. In a sense, the clock was theirs and the Boks were compelled to chase the second hand, sometimes coming close but never being able to actually grasp it. As Claassen told reporters afterwards: 'Our problem lies with the tight five. The question that we have to answer is whether there are better players out there that we can use.'

Much has been made subsequently of the fact that the Springboks needed to make better use of the wind in the first half, but in retrospect this seems spurious. One popular argument has it that had the home team made more telling use of the wind they would not have turned around at 3-all and, as a result, the second half might have been significantly different. This speculation about the wind and the weather is really just criticism of the beleaguered Marais at one remove or, put differently, criticism of his mistaken hope that raw Bok courage would result in an early lead, which could then be defended as the match progressed. He told me that the likes of Coetzee, who should have known about these things because he was a farmer, counselled that the wind would ease off as evening approached. The choice to play with it was therefore a way of having the best of both worlds. It did not quite turn out like this, and Marais, the man who had lifted stones on the beach road in the autumn to get fit, unfairly became the single most important cause of his team's defeat.

'Today he [Marais] must be a disillusioned man,' wrote Rod Hartman in Monday's *Rand Daily Mail*. 'He was buckled in the scrums by "Mighty Mouse" McLauchlan, was unable to keep up with his younger opponents in the loose and failed to inspire his side.' The Marais debate had a full week to mature, because the side for the second Test was only announced after the Lions versus Transvaal game the following Saturday. The name on everyone's lips as the most likely candidate to replace Marais as captain was that of the gallant young Du Plessis.

For Giliomee, one image from that first Test has lingered. He remembers watching Boland Coetzee, the Maties flank, using his hand to stabilise himself in a scrum. As the Lions pack shoved the Boks backwards, so Coetzee's fingers slithered through the mud, unable to find traction. This ghastly image of weakness, the ultimate humiliation for a rugby nation that prided itself on the strength of its scrum, is worth reflecting upon. The Lions did not only win the Newlands Test and the Test series 3-0, as well as all the provincial games, but wherever they went in the beloved country, they pushed the Boks backwards into rugby darkness, into the pre-history from whence Claassen the colossus had come. 'South African rugby is standing still' was a refrain often read and frequently heard during the Lions tour, yet the description is inaccurate. South African rugby devolved during the series; it *actively* went backwards, its lowest point coming in the shambles that was the second Test, in Pretoria, Afrikanerdom's political, if not spiritual, home. Indeed, such devolution gave new meaning to the phrase 'hitting rock bottom'.

Other than the swaying posts and Windsor's menacing verbal assault on his opposite number, Coetzee being driven through the mud is one of the indelible images of the Test. Had it not been for F.C.B. Mellish, the Springbok manager for the Newlands Test, it might have been worse. In his post-Test report to Alex Kellermann, the SA board secretary, he drew attention to the fact that the Boks were not as savvy about the conditions as they should have been. 'It is indeed surprising that players of international standard should be ill-prepared as far as their boots are concerned. Some of the players' boots were inadequately studded and these had to be attended to. Fortunately we had the services of the Olympic Footwear Manufacturers Ltd who attended to the needs of the players in respect of their goods.'

*

Morné du Plessis' résumé looks suspiciously like that of many Springbok players and captains – Grey College, Stellenbosch University, Western Province – but it repays closer scrutiny because what lies in the shadows is more significant than what is bathed in light. Despite being the son of a Springbok captain – his dad Felix captained the 1949 Boks – there was a generous spread of influences in his early life. His mother was a Smethurst and her three brothers, who played football for South Africa, were friends and inspirations. Du Plessis described them in an interview as 'fun guys'. His mom also brought her Presbyterianism and her Englishness into the picture, and from somewhere there came a liberalism and open-heartedness, and a love of cricket, which meant that Du Plessis always stood at a slight angle to the currents of the day. He tells the story of sitting in the Springbok bus at Loftus Versfeld before the second Test against the Lions, for example, and noticing that the Lions were singing while the Bok bus was *tjoepstil.* It led him to wonder if the virtues of Test rugby were not perhaps overrated. 'It was lockdown for us,' he said. 'Our bus was a funeral procession. You wouldn't have dared crack a smile. They were happy and singing and I thought to myself: "There has to be more to rugby than this?" The Western Province teams in those days were student teams and we were bordering on naughty, so I was beginning to think about these sorts of things.'

To call Du Plessis a misfit and a rebel is to overstate things considerably, but, at the same time, he was never quite grave enough about life as a Bok for the authorities to be entirely comfortable with him. While the stern men in green blazers suspected an unhealthy liking for life after the final whistle, especially as a young man, the players certainly held him in high regard. As Bayvel said in his inimitably colourful way: 'The Northerns boys just didn't like the fancy boys from the south. Morné could do it hard *and* play around. They respected him.'

Still, the establishment had their reservations. Although he had travelled with Claassen and Marais to Australia in 1971 ('He had been with us in the wilderness,' said Claassen), there was a worrying recklessness to his personality, and sometimes his play. Craven had warned in his book, *Die ABC van Rugby*, that you never changed a captain in mid-series, and the wise men were inclined to agree. The press were getting bolshie, admittedly, but although Marais had been exposed by McLauchlan in the first Test, things would hopefully get better. It was wiser, surely, to change Marais' front row and help him that way, rather than elevating Du Plessis to captain. Changing captains might backfire horribly. And it was not as though Du Plessis had had a great game himself at Newlands.

Sometime in early 1974, Du Plessis and his University of Cape Town (UCT) mate, the maverick Dugald MacDonald, managed to get hold of a projector. The film of the Barbarians match against the All Blacks at Cardiff Arms Park was circulating among Cape Town's ambitious young rugby players and they desperately wanted to see *that* Edwards try, possibly more than once, and *that* Bennett step as, Houdini-like, he manages to evade the falling net of All Black tacklers. 'We had a projector somewhere and we played the sequence [starting with Bennett and finishing with Edwards] about a hundred times,' remembered Du Plessis. 'They were the Muhammad Alis of the world game at that stage. Dugald and I and the Western Province boys all watched that film. We couldn't get enough of it.'

It was a complicated time to be a young rugby player in the Western Cape. They knew themselves to be different – they were not, for example, the dour, unsmiling practitioners from the north – but at the same time they did not quite know who or what they were. They were certainly boisterous and full of bullshit and, at times, wildly over-exuberant. On occasion, like on the '71 tour of Australia, they must have drained Claassen's fabled reserves of tranquillity until the pool was almost dry. Although Peter Cronje was not a Province player, he was roughly the same age as Du Plessis and MacDonald, and, like Du Plessis, was on the '71 tour. When it came to pursuing life off the field, Cronje behaved as any good outside centre should, happily going in search of every available outside gap. At one point Claassen had a word. So did a deeply reluctant Frik du Preez, the then Bok captain. According to Cronje, their exchange went something like this:

> 'So Prof has had a word with you?'
>
> 'Ja, Frik, he's had a word.'
>
> 'So you know what this is about?'
>
> 'I do. And by the way, I don't drink brandy, Frik; can't stand the bloody stuff.'
>
> 'That's not for you, Cronje, it's for me.'

MacDonald was even more out there than the likeable wild boy, Cronje; he was a philosopher and a thinker, full of ideas and theorising, and hungry for knowledge, but not quite the finished article as a small but storming number 8. Legend has it that he arrived at the airport to go on the Gazelles' 1972 tour of Argentina with no more luggage than a small, cheap suitcase. Once there, he survived on soup, stubbornly refusing to eat the famous Argentine trinchados. 'He rocks up with this tiny suitcase,' remembered Bayvel. 'In it he's got a toothbrush and some shaving kit and a pair of running shorts and takkies. That's about it. We've got our kit and number ones and blazers. Dugald was something else, truly special.'

MacDonald told me in an interview that there was a dim awareness when the Lions arrived in South Africa that 'we were getting into something we hadn't bargained for'. Looking back through my notes, the word he used to describe the feeling was 'trepidation', which suggests that there was a forewarning or premonition beforehand – at some inchoate or unconscious level everyone recognised the looming crisis. '*The Lions Speak* by J.G.B. Thomas was a book about their victory in New Zealand in 1971,' MacDonald told me. 'It was a technical book and it had chapters by Carwyn James, David Duckham, Gerald Davies, John Taylor. If you took that and compared it to the knowledge of South African rugby at the time, you will realise that they were on a different planet. If you read it you will begin to grasp the difference between the Lions and where we were. The book wasn't available here. We somehow got a copy at UCT and we all asked: "Where do these guys come from? Who are they?" We were just mesmerised.'

MacDonald scored the only try for Southern Universities in their 4-26 defeat by the Lions at Newlands on the Tuesday following the first Test. The Western Cape rugby public could not get enough of the men from overseas; although the weather was still grim and it was a midweek game, 20 000 fans packed into the stadium to watch the visitors score four tries, three of them by forwards (Brown, Kennedy and Uttley). So dire and grinding was the victory, though, that McBride felt compelled to offer a sort of apology, despite the fact that McLauchlan captained the team against the combined universities. 'This was a victory for the players,' McBride told the press, the implication being that 'winning dirty' was, in both senses of the phrase, preferable to throwing the ball around. The Lions' pragmatism and correct assessment of the type of rugby appropriate to the conditions suggested that they would transport such methods on their voyage north. After the game against Southern Universities, the papers were full of the familiar refrain that the Lions were perverting the romance of the game. The bleating led to the prediction that the Lions – who had conquered the Cape and dealt with everything the four sides could throw at them – were likely to take their dull '*wenrugby*' upcountry. It could not have been further from the truth.

The game brought the Lions' journey in the south to an end. Many in South Africa had predicted that their first defeat would come either at the hands of Western Province or the Springboks – or both. It was not to be. In fact, it was all getting a little worrying. A group of Transvaal Rugby Union (TRU) administrators watched the first Test and did not like what they saw. They predicted that, unless Transvaal managed to beat the visitors, there was a strong likelihood that the Lions would march through southern Africa without losing. People both within the rugby establishment and without were now actively concerned. South African rugby did not seem to be as strong as everyone had assumed. The technical aspects of forward play seemed to have been neglected, and the Springboks had now gone 160 minutes of Test rugby (if one counted the Pullin Test in '72) without scoring a try.

The Southern Universities game also threw up a worrying little addendum. Newlands was invaded – if invaded is the word – by three left-wing protesters, the first ever on a South African sports field. The protesters, two boys and a girl, met their match, when an incensed spectator stabbed the girl in the eye with his umbrella. The incident was significant enough to be recorded by

Visser, who said: '*Vir die eerste keer by 'n rugbywedstryd in Suid-Afrika is daar betoog deur 'n klomp studente.*' (For the first time in a rugby match in South Africa there was a demonstration by a group of students.) Some of rugby's natives were getting restless. The Newlands incident was not to be the only time South African crowds would get uppity on the Lions tour.

*

Two weeks before the tourists arrived in South Africa, a group of left-wing officers overthrew Portugal's right-wing military regime in what came to be known as the Carnation Revolution. The significance of the bloodless coup was not immediately apparent to South Africans, but in time diplomats, political scientists and journalists, as well as the power brokers in Pretoria and the exiled elite, became acutely aware of the implications of the takeover. This was because the officers made it clear that one of their objectives was to sever Portugal's 500-year colonial ties with Africa. Portugal's African colonies (Angola, Mozambique and Cape Verde) were to be offered their independence and it was likely to happen sooner rather than later.

In one fell swoop, John Vorster, the South African prime minister who had returned a National Party majority in the elections earlier in the year, looked out on a changed geopolitical landscape. The states surrounding South Africa were now falling, one by one, leaving only Rhodesia as an ally. The implications were not lost on the *The Star*'s political correspondent, Wilf Nussey. 'No event since World War 2 has accelerated the course of African events and the cause of African nationalism more dramatically than the April 25 coup in Portugal,' he wrote in the newspaper's weekend edition of 1 June. 'In five swift weeks it has stripped away the comforting security of Mozambique and Angola, shaken to the foundations the delicate co-existence between black and white states throughout southern Africa, drastically bruised the white and boosted the black morale, and thrown the future into huge doubt. It could be a year, possibly more, before the full shock is felt of the tremendous psychological, political, racial and administrative turbulence this 20th century Jericho has created in Portuguese Africa ... At the worst South Africa will find herself totally isolated and alone, beset along its land borders by guerrillas, harassed internally by sanctions – a last, dogged and vilified laager of white supremacy.'

Another article in that Saturday's newspaper discussed the subject of landing rights for South African aircraft in Portugal's independent colonies. Neville Barber, the journalist concerned, believed it likely that newly elected governments in Angola and the Cape Verde islands would 'think again about allowing SAA [South African Airways] landing rights on flights to Europe'. According to Barber, SAA was 'watching the situation closely', which indeed it was, because at about the same time SAA started placing a simple but effective advert in South African newspapers. No more than 200 mm tall and perhaps 150 mm wide, the advert listed 20 European capitals and destinations in alphabetical order from top to bottom down the page. Across the page, from left to right, were listed the days of the week, with the vertical and horizontal axes intersecting, say, twice a week in the case of Athens, three times a week in the case of Frankfurt and four times a week in the case of London, the crosses at the point of intersection indicating the number of times per week that SAA flew to said destination. The heading of the advert was a simple 'We get you there'. In the face of mounting international disapproval, SAA was keeping pathways into the Old World open. It was a version of the Lions coming to South Africa in reverse.

The national carrier's marketing department was playing upon exactly the same white fears that were coursing through South Africa's rugby establishment. The Lions tour was vital because it lent credibility to South African rugby and the country at large. In a narrower sense it also sanctioned – if only implicitly – rugby's guarded efforts at reform in the shape of matches at the Goodwood Showgrounds and, later, against the Leopards in Mdantsane. Marais spoke to me about the Springboks' need to give a good account of themselves, because, if they did not, there were inchoate fears that the Lions would not come back, as it would not be worth their while in rugby terms to do so. The problem for the rugby players was not the moral and political one of apartheid. Their problem was expressed in far narrower terms: sporting underachievement. This, in part, was why the series defeat, and the terraced symbolism of that defeat, was so difficult for the rugby establishment to digest. The anti-apartheid activists, the left-wing politicians and the liberal world in general did not bother them unduly; neither were they overly concerned by what these linked constituencies might do by way of boycotts and isolation. Primarily, the Boks were unsettled by the spectre of sporting failure, the ghost that hovered over their game throughout the tour. If they lost the series, they opened up the possibility that their worst fears might be realised. It was almost a self-fulfilling prophecy in that what Claassen, Marais, Craven and others most feared is exactly what came to pass.

5

Running rugby on the Highveld

THE ICONOGRAPHY AND language of South African rugby in 1974 was startlingly different to what we have today. Western Transvaal were called the *mielieboere*, a phrase miraculously still in use, but who nowadays remembers the *vol-struisboere*, as South Western Districts were lovingly called in the more sentimentally inclined sections of the Afrikaans press? If you wanted to know about rugby, you either watched the game live or read about it in your newspaper of choice. The back sections of both the daily and weekend papers were crammed with coverage, partly the consequence of a competitive market and partly because television only arrived in South Africa 18 months later, at the beginning of 1976. In both English and Afrikaans newspaper groups, regional bureaus were still a feature of life. Coverage was wide and readers were spoilt for choice. If you wanted to read about the Lions in *The Star*, for instance, a copy of the newspaper would set you back all of seven cents. It was a golden age for South African broadsheets.

Rugby stadiums in the period were pre-modern and uncomfortable. Despite their size, they were frequently slightly worse for wear and sometimes had an almost rustic feel. Spectators spilt onto the touchline, linesmen wore buttoned-up blazers and there was only one type of rugby ball, the Super Springbok, produced by Invincible Industries of Elsies River in the Western Cape. Scoreboards were manual, naartjies were juicy and if you nursed it with appropriate care, a *stuk* of kudu biltong would last the entire second half. A referee's boots were perfectly polished, the folds in his socks could be measured with a spirit level and his hair was slicked into a side parting with crisp authority. Such were the signs of the times. From a distance it seems that we are almost in the realm of a South African rugby gothic. The portrait is painted by Andrew Wyeth and shows Hannes Marais standing in front of a barn, a pitchfork in his hand, a weather-beaten woman by his side.

Some provincial executives acknowledged that their stadiums could do with more than a fresh lick of paint. In 1969, under their president, Jannie le Roux, members of the TRU undertook the first of two round-the-world trips to see how stadiums were built and refurbished elsewhere. It was only in 1979, however, 10 years after their first voyage (they somehow managed to smuggle in a detour to New York on one of the junkets) and nearly 15 years after Le Roux became president, that the union finally received permission from the Johannesburg City Council to go ahead with rebuilding Ellis Park. Completed in 1982 – the official opening was on 15 May 1982 – it was Le Roux's last significant administrative act before passing the Super Springbok to Louis Luyt.

Le Roux was not a man without Stellenbosch connections. An attorney by profession, he had played flyhalf for the Maties first XV and in 1972 became Craven's vice-president on the SA board. His ascension to the vice-presidency was coloured by regret for Craven, because while in many ways Le Roux was his blue-eyed boy, the decision meant getting rid of the older Kobus Louw, a valued member of Craven's inner sanctum. 'Craven felt very sorry for Mr Louw, but his favourite was Le Roux,' Herman le Roux of *Volksblad* told me. 'He wondered if perhaps he pushed the old stalwart out too quickly and whether he'd made a mistake. I remember this all because I asked him about it at a break in a meeting once. We were both at the buffet and he looked pensive. I think he wasn't completely comfortable with the decision.'

The SARB vice-president had a cosy sinecure as Transvaal president because he owned a Doornfontein bottle store close to Ellis Park that supplied the union with all its liquor needs. His rationale, according to Mike Shafto, was that there was no way beer trucks could cause a bottleneck (as it were) around headquarters as they were offloading. Far better, Le Roux explained, for his liquor store to supply the Ellis Park function rooms and kitchens. It was less visible, smoother and caused far less congestion.

Luyt, meanwhile, was making his millions and keeping his gunpowder dry. Indeed, halfway through 1974, reports started surfacing in the press of a highly lucrative export deal for South African fertiliser. The two main actors were the Phosphate Development Corporation (Foskor), represented by J.P. Kearney, and Luyt himself, chairman of the Triomf fertiliser factory. Overseas orders were reputed to be in the region of R1.3 billion and Luyt was anxious to transport his fertiliser to the coast as quickly as possible. 'Mr Luyt said yesterday that negotiations were underway with the SA Railways on the means of transporting 3000 tonnes a day of phosphate concentrate from the Foskor works in Phalaborwa to Richard's Bay,' wrote Chris

Cairncross in the *Business Mail* supplement to the *Rand Daily Mail* on 15 June.

Bankrolled by his fertiliser millions and fuelled by a hankering for an administrative role in a game he had played with distinction over 50 times for the Orange Free State, Luyt was only a peripheral figure in rugby circles in the mid-seventies. By the early 1980s, however, he was ready to pounce, using what from afar looks suspiciously like back-slapping chumminess of the worst kind. Luyt, who was handily placed because Le Roux had done at least some of his work for him in modernising Ellis Park, for instance, understood that rugby needed to be weaned off its amateur ethos. Players had to be properly compensated for the brutalities of the sport; television moguls needed to be courted; and the game's financial status needed to be elevated. With Luyt's arrival on the scene, so Craven's administrative days were, in a sense, numbered. It might have taken almost a decade, but either by stealth or steamroller, Luyt eventually ushered in local rugby's professional age.

All that was yet to come. In the seventies, Luyt was simply the ruthless hyena pacing hungrily on the wrong side of the perimeter fence. While he was shovelling away his fortune, club rugby remained the bedrock of the domestic game in the Transvaal. One of the cornerstones of the scene was Diggers Rugby Club, with their famous grounds at Springfield, just off Eloff Street Extension in southern Johannesburg. As suggested by its name, Diggers started as a club for the rugby-playing miners and white-collar professionals of the Rand. As such, they were similar to other Reef clubs with gold-mining beginnings like Simmer & Jack, West Rand Consolidated and Crown Mines, although they were by far the most successful of the four. Diggers' mining history is represented on the club's coat of arms – an animal-hide fighting shield in front of two partially obscured assegais, with a pick, shovel and rugby ball depicted on the shield itself. Founded in 1893, at first the club was predominantly English-speaking, but in the years leading up to the Second World War it became strongly Afrikaans and family based. The change in composition culminated in a legendary court action in 1944 against the then English-dominated TRU, which, the Diggers executive believed, was not acting with sufficient sensitivity towards their Afrikaans-speaking interests.

By the late sixties and early seventies, Diggers was in its prime. For the 1974 club season, Anton Oberholzer took over the club captaincy from the legendary Piet Greyling, and the club was full of Boks and Boks-to-be, including Bayvel, De Klerk, Sauermann and Cronje. Oberholzer, who captained Transvaal against the Lions, remembers his days at Springfield with great fondness. It was never a place of superb amenities, he told me, but the club was populated by an array of characters and there was a great team spirit and sense of belonging. 'There was a bar close by called the Split Poles; no alcohol was actually served at Springfield,' he recalled. 'We had change rooms, a caretaker's house and a meeting room under the caretaker's house and a tuck shop. We had three fields and you went there to play rugby. There were sheep grazing on the far fields sometimes. Those dome lights that we had were so low that when the ball was kicked up at night it just disappeared, you couldn't see a thing. I remember after the Lions game against Transvaal at Ellis Park we all just trooped down to Springfield for an ox braai and a few beers.'

One of the legends of Springfield was Jim Foley, the first-XV coach. By day Foley was in the roofing business; by night he put on his tracksuit, grabbed his whistle and made for practice. 'Jim was one of the most wonderful guys out,' Oberholzer told me. 'If there was any trouble on the field he used to yell "*Stitch hulle*" from the touchline – give them a short-arm jab. He used to believe in *maagspiere*, so the forwards were always doing stomach exercises. That was his big thing.'

Paul Bayvel was a contemporary of Oberholzer's at Diggers. He was introduced to the club by his Parktown Boys High schoolmate Peter Cronje (the two played together in an unbeaten Parktown Boys first XV in 1968), who told him that at Diggers he would get adequate protection at scrumhalf, unlike at Wits, where he had had his collarbone broken twice in two seasons. 'The Wits thing didn't really happen for me and I wasn't much of a student, so I moved across [to Diggers],' Bayvel told me. 'We were coached by this real hard-ass called Foley. It didn't matter who you were, you always started in the club's second XV. Moaner [van Heerden] arrived at the club one year and caught the ball after kickoff, as he always did, and started charging towards me. I took one look at this and just waved him by like a traffic policeman. Afterwards I'm thinking: "Shit, that maybe wasn't the smartest thing to do." It was only then that I noticed Foley behind the posts, screaming with laughter.'

Oberholzer was never as mean as Van Heerden and never quite as *windgat* as the young Bayvel. Although he was comparatively small for a number 8, he had an uncomplaining temperament, a big heart and huge lungs. When others were fading in the last quarter he came into his own, if anything becoming stronger as the clock ran down. It meant that coaches loved him and it played no small part in him becoming captain after Greyling. He was never quite big or good enough to be a Springbok, he told me, although that did not prevent him from playing in three Currie Cup finals ('71, '72 and '74), drawing with Northern Transvaal in 1971 and beating Eastern Transvaal in 1972. Perks in those days were not quite up to the standard of today's sponsored Subaru Sprinter, so in two of the three finals Oberholzer took home nothing more than a free tracksuit and a massive *babbelas*.

In our interview I was struck by Oberholzer's almost noble love of the game, a love, it should be pointed out, frequently sprinkled with mischief. He told me that after matriculating from Jeppe Boys High and spending nearly a year doing little else but playing rugby at the Naval College at Gordon's Bay, he went up to the University of Pretoria, or Tukkies, to do an agricultural degree. He fought his way into the Tukkies under-20 side and from there graduated to Northerns under-20. Rugby in Pretoria at the time was dirty, physical and hugely enjoyable; Oberholzer has no doubt his time there was the making of him as a player. 'The old Police and Army guys had come out of first league,' he told me from the warmth of a Portuguese restaurant near his old school on a cold day in July 2013. 'They were hardened warriors. It was very tough; they knew all the tricks. It used to be a riot. It was fantastic rugby.'

In the week prior to the Transvaal match against the Lions, Oberholzer was reunited with his mate Sakkie Sauermann, who had been roughed up by Fran Cotton at Newlands in the first Test. Sauermann was a worried man because technically he had experienced the might of the Lions pack. They were clever, he told his captain, and did things he had never experienced before.

'Sakkie told us all about "the squeeze", so we were prepared for it,' Oberholzer told me. 'The Lions had this call on the opposition's ball in which they squeezed their pack. It wasn't like today where you have the touch-pause-engage thing; the scrums in those days hit each other and the Lions squeezed tight. On the call they would move ever so slightly to the left or the right to get their opponents off-balance, and then there would be this *moerse* shove. Of course Sakkie came back and told us all about this, so we had a couple of things up our sleeve.'

Over the course of the tour a rhythm was established whereby the Lions' next major provincial encounter was seen by the scribes as the expression of a final rearguard for the home team – a Western Province, a Transvaal or an Orange Free State – with the win hopefully ushering in a period of improved fortunes for the national side. The Transvaal match followed exactly this logic, with pundits and fans understanding the game (or, more specifically, representing the game) in heroic last-chance-saloon terms more appropriate, say, to a Spaghetti Western at the local bioscope. Transvaal were not, therefore, only playing for provincial pride; they ended up shouldering the increasingly heavy and confused burdens of South African rugby. 'Unless they are beaten or at least well held by Transvaal at Ellis Park on Saturday the British Lions will steamroller through the rest of their tour without defeat in either provincial games or the remaining Test matches,' wrote Shafto in *The Star* shortly before the Transvaal match. 'This is the gloomy view of most of the Transvaal Rugby union committee who travelled down to Cape Town en masse to see the Springboks beaten 12-3 in the first Test at Newlands last weekend.'

In his on-day preview, Hartman struck a similarly sober

note. 'The Lions tour reaches a high point this afternoon when almost 40 000 Transvaal supporters go to Ellis Park hoping desperately for the downfall of Willie John McBride's team,' he wrote in the *Rand Daily Mail*. 'South African rugby is in a state of near panic as the Lions sweep unbeaten towards the second Test. The message has gone out to Anton Oberholzer's team: "Save our rugby".'

The prevailing mood was plunged into an even deeper shade of grey when, on the Friday night, it became known that naartjie-sellers at Ellis Park were to be outlawed on match day. No explanation was given, but it meant that at least some of the expected 40 000 fans would be deprived of juice and traditional ammunition. Pre-match fare, explained stadium catering manager Peter Coetzee, would be confined to roughly 80 000 pies, hamburgers and hotdogs. This, doubtless, resulted in a quandary for hardcore fans who came to the rugby expressly to throw naartjies. A pie would disintegrate before hitting its target and hamburgers and hotdogs were aerodynamically suspect. Besides, having forked out for a burger or hotdog, was it advisable to get rid of it immediately by hurling it at the referee? What would happen to the bun? Would the mustard relish dribble down the collar of the man three rows in front and, if so, would he *bliksem* the thrower? These were important questions, although they paled into insignificance when compared to the bigger question of what the Lions' first-Test front row of McLauchlan, Windsor and Cotton would do to *Rooibontes* meanies Johan Strauss, Dave Frederickson and Sakkie himself. To add drama to the impending front-row battle, the scribes were thin-slicing some of the match-ups. At first blush, McLauchlan versus Strauss did not look like much of a contest:

Strauss was 1.8 metres tall and weighed 104 kilograms to the Scot's 1.7 metres and modest 91 kilos. The most telling stat, though, was in their respective ages: at 32, the 'Mighty Mouse' was a scrumming veteran, while poor Strauss was an experiential lightweight – as it were – at 10 years his junior. It was going to be a hot afternoon down in the bowels of the beast.

On game day, the fun and games extended onto the Ellis Park pitch. After winning the toss and choosing ends, Oberholzer led his side out to find the Lions already warming up in the Transvaal half. Unperturbed, he simply squeezed round them, indicating to referee Piet Robbertse that the Lions should change ends because Transvaal had choice of ends, as they had called correctly. At halftime, perhaps a little surprisingly, they were 9-3 to the good, their points coming from three Gerald Bosch penalties to Bennett's one.

It was a big game for Bosch and his halfback partner, Bayvel. Bosch was the ultimate kicking flyhalf and it was felt that after Dawie Snyman's iffy performance at Newlands, he might just nudge into the frame for the second Test. The Bosch issue was not without its complications. The Loftus Test the week after the Transvaal game would be played on a hard, fast surface under clear winter skies; the ideal situation, in other words, for running rugby if the Bok pack was able to win sufficient good ball. In which case Bosch was perhaps not the answer. In the end, it did not matter. With the exception of McGeechan, Steele, Edwards, Slattery and Davies, the Lions fielded the same team that had played in the Test at Newlands, including Bennett at flyhalf, J.J. Williams on the wing and McBride and Brown as the locks. The replacements were not half bad either. Tony Neary on the openside flank was ideally suited to the dry and quick Ellis Park surface because of his speed, and Andy Ripley was as good a player, many felt, as Davies at number 8. The Lions selectors also continued with their successful Newlands experiment of playing Uttley as Neary's partner on the flank. He offered another lineout option and his bulk was a useful antidote to both Neary's comparative lack of size and the fact that Transvaal were playing with a traditionally monster-sized pack, with Salty du Rand adding bulk in the second row along-side the massive Kevin de Klerk.

As the match progressed, so matters soured for the home side and their naartjie-deprived supporters. The Lions put in their by now characteristically muscular second-half performance, uncorking the fizz of their loose forwards and backs, who scored three tries through J.P.R. Williams, Neary and Dick Milliken. Despite their best intentions and the hopes of the public and the press, it was a startlingly anticlimactic performance from Transvaal, a fact not lost on Oberholzer, who watched his side leak 20 points after the halftime whistle. 'I asked Willie John at the post-match function what he'd said to his side at halftime,' he told me. 'Remember, we were the only side to have a halftime lead against them in the entire series, and he replied by telling me: "We have this saying in Ireland that if you sit on the pot you must either shit or get off, so I told them either play or don't bother. I haven't come for you to lose to Transvaal in the week before the second Test, so let's get on with it or get off."'

Any hoped-for clarifications post the Transvaal match were slow to emerge and the selectors sat for hours afterwards before announcing the side for Loftus. In the end they resisted the temptation to drop Marais, instead favouring two front-row changes: Dave Frederickson, the Transvaal hooker, replaced

Piston van Wyk after a good game that afternoon against the Lions, and Niek Bezuidenhout, the Northern Transvaal loosehead, replaced Sauermann. Bezuidenhout's selection looked particularly questionable. On the same afternoon that Transvaal played the Lions, Northern Transvaal took on Natal, with Piet Nieman playing instead of him in the Northerns' front row. In fairness to Bezuidenhout, he was already a Springbok, having played against England in '72, although the consensus was that he had disappointed against Pullin and his men. It was a desperate ploy, although, in mitigation, it was felt that Bezuidenhout was better technically than Sauermann, so he might just be able to provide the answer for which the selectors were so desperately looking. The lock pairing, meanwhile (Williams and De Klerk), remained the same, with the mercurial MacDonald making his Bok debut at eighthman after some consistently good performances for Western Province and Southern Universities. After a mediocre first Test, Boland Coetzee lost his place, Du Plessis going into his position on the flank from the back of the scrum to make way for MacDonald. Many felt it was where Du Plessis was at his best.

The changes in the pack were nothing compared to the wild swinging of the selectorial axe behind it. Both first-Test halfbacks were chopped, Bosch and Bayvel coming in for Dawie Snyman and Roy McCallum; Jackie Snyman of the Orange Free State replaced Johan Oosthuizen in the centre after the latter's jaw injury at Newlands; and, late in the day, Gerrie Germishuys came in for Gert Muller on the wing, the selectors having hoped that Muller would recover from injury in time.

For Bayvel, it was a longer Saturday night than usual. After the post-match function at Springfield, he and Cronje (who played for Transvaal but was not deemed fit enough to be chosen for the second Test) headed to their favourite watering hole at the Sunnyside Hotel in Parktown for a few more toots. They arrived at the flat they shared in Craighall Park past midnight, considerably worse for wear. 'We were blotto, completely shikka,' he said. 'We rocked home and my dad was standing waiting there for us. He'd heard it [the announcement of the side] on the radio and wanted to break the news.'

*

As in South Africa, there was a general election in the United Kingdom in 1974. The February election resulted in a hung parliament, with Harold Wilson's Labour winning more seats than Edward Heath's Conservatives, but not enough to give Labour a clear majority. (This was achieved later in the year when Heath resigned after failing to reach consensus with the Liberal Party's Jeremy Thorpe over the formation of a coalition government.) The new Labour government was publicly opposed to the tour and would have preferred it if the Lions did not travel to South Africa, Wilson's minister of sport, Dennis Howell, saying as much on several occasions beforehand. As the departure date grew closer, they were reluctantly forced to admit that their preferences were being ignored. Other than their political and moral objections, what they feared most was that there would be a backlash from some African and Third World countries, which would refuse sporting ties with Britain in other sporting arenas. The Olympics were in mid-cycle, the 1976 Games being scheduled for Montreal, and Britain was aware of how the New Zealanders had handled the threat to the 1974 Commonwealth Games. In response to what it believed was the rugby administrators' gung-ho attitude, the Foreign Office issued a directive to its embassies and consular officials in South Africa to the effect that they were forbidden to have any formal contact with the tourists once they arrived. At one point it also explored the possibility of revoking the Lions' visas for the midweek match in Salisbury against Rhodesia, the last game before the second Test, but this never happened because it proved to be too ethically dubious. 'The RDM correspondent in London reports that the British government tried with much greater vigour to stop the Rhodesian leg of the Lions tour than the South African section but it did not have the power to officially ban the match in Salisbury,' Hartman wrote in a composite article. '[T]he Government considered closing exchange control facilities for the Lions and even invalidating their passports for Rhodesia. But although Rhodesia is in a state of rebellion, the Labour government could not take these steps without first introducing legislation.'

Peter Hain, who led the movement to have the tour stopped, welcomed the British government's initiative not to permit the tourists consular recognition, suggesting that it was an improvement on their 'pretty fence-sitting record so far'. The wit, however, came from Eldon Griffiths, the former sports minister in Heath's government, who noted – correctly, one suspects – that the Foreign Office's instruction to shun the tourists 'was a spiteful little gesture'. Warming to his theme, he continued: 'That the British Lions will tremble in their boots at the thought of being denied a handshake by the ambassador is surely a trifle ludicrous.'

While the political subtext around the Rhodesia game was deeper and more complicated than usual, in a sense the quick trip north amounted to a veiled bribe: a midweek match against the plucky spirits of Rhodesia in return for a hurried sightseeing trip on the Sunday afternoon to Victoria Falls. Either way, the itinerary was not ideal. It was more travelling than the Lions would have liked ahead of the Test, Mike Gibson still had not arrived and they were uncertain of whom to run at flyhalf, thinking it advisable to keep Bennett and his Welsh dancing shoes in cotton wool. In the end it was McGeechan who played at 10, Edwards captaining the team from the base of the scrum as his partner. Andy Irvine handled the kicking duties from fullback, from where he reeled in a significant haul of 22 points.

For possibly the first time on tour, the Lions selections were self-evidently conservative, with no J.P.R. Williams, no Bennett, no McBride, no Brown, no Windsor and no McLauchlan, all players vital to the functioning spine of the side. As was the case so often on the tour, the Lions did not seem to be unduly weakened, turning on the charm early rather than late in front of 22 000 dazzled Rhodesian spectators and one Springbok selector, Butch Lochner, who had flown up to cast an eye over the Lions' performance ahead of the Loftus Test. In winning 42-6 (25-6 at halftime), the Lions scored six tries, beating Des Christian's men at a modest canter. The post-match reception was at the Police Club in Salisbury and, at around midnight, Milliken, who had probably played his best game so far on tour against Transvaal, lurched out of the function with Windsor in search of fresh air. Parked close by was a limousine and, lo and behold, the keys were in the ignition. Neither could refuse the opportunity and jumped in; so excited were they to drive a limo and test its capabilities that neither noticed the glass-frosted partition between the front and back seats. Milliken and Windsor were enjoying themselves so much driving at hell-or-glory speeds along the sleepy streets of the Rhodesian capital that it was some time before they noticed that the partition had been opened from the back. 'You gentlemen seem to be having so much fun, I wonder if you wouldn't like to come and work for me,' came a voice from deep inside. They turned to see Ian Smith, the prime minister, sitting there with a big smile on his face.

Irvine's performance against the Rhodesians caused some head-scratching among the Lions selectors. They met twice on Tuesday before announcing their side at a press conference at their Pretoria hotel after having returned from Salisbury on the Wednesday. Many felt Irvine, with his speed and superior long boot, should replace Steele on the wing. As it was, the Lions side for the second Test remained identical to the side that had won the first. There was an outside possibility that Chris Ralston might just force his way past Gordon Brown in the second row, but the Scot had scored four important tries going into the second Test and it was felt his contribution in the lineout and the loose outweighed that of the Englishman's. As it was, the South African pressmen were not disappointed. They favoured Irvine over Steele, so were not too concerned when the Lions remained unchanged. Hope was increasingly hard to find, so they clung to whatever flotsam the great sea of tour news would bring.

No phase of the tour has attracted so much brightly embroidered blarney as have the days leading up to the second Test in Pretoria. Documentaries featuring respected Lions have not only told of the Boks living in jail from the Wednesday beforehand, but have added mischievously that the post-match function was also spent in prison, the meal doubtlessly being slopped into mess trays and eaten with institutional cutlery. Without perhaps being fully aware of the images they were creating, the tellers have done their best to represent the Springboks as sporting automatons in a crazed totalitarian empire, a sort of Soviet bloc meets the veld with the Voortrekker monument loitering in the background. Superficially it is a compelling tale and it squares with one's idea of the Boks' chastised, head-down beleaguered-ness. Of course this does not make the lurid tales true, but rather tells of the ways in which the victors have happily embellished history in the ways they have seen fit.

Stories have, for instance, circulated to the effect that Dimitri Tsafendas, the Greek schizophrenic imprisoned for stabbing Hendrik Verwoerd, served the Springboks tea and biscuits at practice before the Test. Other yarns have recounted how the Boks lived in isolation in the days leading up to Loftus, with outside visitors and press intrusion being kept to a minimum. As with all fabrications, such stories have been magnified over time, taking on a healthily independent life of their own.

In contrast, the bare facts of the days leading up to the Loftus Test are as follows. The Springboks trained at Baviaanspoort Correctional Services, a tightly controlled prison environment to which journalists were not allowed access. They gathered a day early, on the Wednesday before the game rather than the Thursday, as was usually the case. They lived in an inner-city hotel, with curfews in the evenings, and they were discouraged from reading the papers or having too much contact with the outside world. The atmosphere was more tense than usual, certainly, and more humourless, although the rituals of practice matches, team talks, a film viewing of the first Test and chats to individual players were very much in evidence.

Enterprising as ever, the journalists still managed to find out what Claassen told the players, particularly the new Boks, and gleefully reported it. To Jackie Snyman he brought the news that he had been incredibly close to being named as a reserve for the 1969/70 tour to the United Kingdom, and that although he was now the Orange Free State flyhalf, he should use his experience of six years at centre to show the Lions exactly what he could do. From John Williams, the lock, Claassen asked for more fire; he told MacDonald to translate his domestic form into form for the Boks; to Germishuys, a debutant like MacDonald, he said that although he had not been picked for the Junior Springboks earlier in the year in any matches on their three-match internal tour, the fact that he had been named as reserve for the first Test was a demonstration that he was highly regarded and was in the selectors' thoughts.

Germishuys's parents could not watch their son play rugby. His dad was a shift worker at Lever Brothers and his mom worked as a studio photographer at Stella Nova on the East Rand on weekends. In a sense there had been no need to watch him, because he'd only played second-team rugby at school and there was little recognition in the family that they might be living with a future Springbok. When he was in junior school, his grandfather, who was a senator in the government, took him aside and told him it did not make good long-term sense to remain a wing. '"Go and play scrumhalf," he told me. "You're too small for a wing." I only really grew bigger in matric and in the army. Up until matric I'd only ever been to Ellis Park once. I played year to year, team to team. I realised if I made the

Transvaal under-20 side then maybe I'd have an opportunity to play for the senior side the next season. That was how it went for me – that was very much my approach.'

Whether out of stubbornness or incipient self-knowledge, Germishuys never took his grandfather's advice. It did not really matter, because by the time he was in his early 20s, the rugby environment was at its most open in years. There had been no tours since Australia in 1971 and the subsequent wave of retirements from players like Du Preez and Greyling had meant that there were no Springbok incumbents and therefore no established pecking order. The selectors might have been none the wiser, but the extension of their cluelessness was that domestic rugby during the period was virgin territory, the proverbial land of hope and opportunity. Germishuys was a reserve for the first Test, but injuries to Muller and Leon Vogel opened the door shortly before the second. He was rushed to Pretoria from Bloemfontein (where he was studying for a teaching degree and playing for Orange Free State) and, although he was incredibly excited, in retrospect it seems a little as if he was a seaman joining the crew of a cursed ship. 'It was doomed from the beginning,' he told me while nursing a tankard of beer at a Northcliff steakhouse in the winter of 2013. 'I really believe we had the players. I believe we weren't coached enough beforehand. You can't get together three days before a Test and expect to be a proper team.'

Germishuys, like many other players from that time, narrates his Loftus experiences without rancour. Finger pointing and a change in the tone of his voice to denote frustration and anger are startlingly absent. If anything, his primary emotion is one of personal underachievement, as though he were forced, through no fault of his own, to leave a highly visible job incomplete. 'You open your eyes, you close your eyes and you open them again and the Test is over,' he said. 'You still want to do something.'

This lingering sense of unfinished business is not confined to the debut winger, who barely touched the ball in 80 minutes of play. In winning the second Test 28-9, the Lions played very much as they wanted to play. By contrast, the Springboks were unable to play as they would have liked, partly because of their under-preparation and partly because of the fact that they were never in control and so could not dictate the pattern or pace of the match. For Germishuys it was a debut clouded by disappointment and underachievement, but he was a young man and would doubtlessly get another chance. Men like Marais were not so lucky. He would have a noble career retrospectively coloured by games like the second Test. There were others still, like MacDonald, Frederickson and Sauermann, who would only ever play once or play in a handful of games long since forgotten. For some of them the path to peace was long and difficult.

It is tempting to see the respective teams' preparations and pre-Test rituals as opposites: the Boks were frigid and frightened; the Lions were happy, confident and aroused. The tourists sang on their bus journey to the ground, their song still in progress when they arrived at the back of the main Loftus grandstand. Instead of stopping short of 'Flower of Scotland', which by now had become their team song, the bus waited and they continued singing. The Boks filed into their dressing room with heavy limbs and a sense of foreboding; the Lions stepped off their bus with a buoyant sense of well-being. They were to play one of the greatest games the red jersey had ever seen and they were to do it in a citadel, a place where visiting teams seldom won and, if they did, only by sustaining injuries to their men and their pride.

*

Seen through the Lions' eyes, Loftus Versfeld represented everything that was alien to their rugby culture, an intimidating place full of fans either actually or implicitly hostile towards them. It was a big stadium, its stands rising like sheer walls from ground level, and it was filled with mainly Afrikaans supporters in what was a predominantly Afrikaans city. The field itself was bleached white from winter frosts; the sun was shining; there was none of the grim, battlefield muddiness associated with the sport in Britain and the weather in which the northern-hemisphere game was usually played.

The hard fields and blue skies proved to be a dilemma for the scribes. Although the Transvaal game showed the Lions could run, no one seemed to trust that this would be the case in the raised stakes of Test rugby. The reporters should not have been so naive. They should have realised that the tourists were nothing if not pragmatic: they would allow the weather and the condition of the field to at least partly dictate how they were going to play. After all, in Bennett, Edwards and the two Williamses, they had men with diamonds on the soles of their shoes. Loftus was the place where they had come to shine.

The Lions pounced early, a marginally offside J.J. Williams darting after a blindside kick by Edwards from the base of the scrum, outstripping Whipp and Ian McCallum to score the first, nerve-settling try. Herman le Roux has the try preserved in his mind's eye all these years later: 'I can still remember Gareth telling J.J. that he's going to send up a little kick and he had all the time he needed to do so. That was a catastrophic Test for us, catastrophic.'

Blindside gaps had clearly been a subject for discussion in the Lions camp, because their third try also came from a blindside break, the move having started on the far side of the field when a Windsor throw into the lineout failed to find its jumper. Jan Ellis used one of his big hands to control the ball and he shovelled it to Jackie Snyman, who gave an intelligent inside pass to Dugald MacDonald, who was loitering on his shoulder; MacDonald was scragged and a ruck was formed. The ball was slow to emerge, but watching the replay the viewer expects the ball eventually – if cumbersomely – to find its way back to Bayvel, the Bok scrumhalf. Instead, the ball fell onto the ground and was worked loose and shovelled out on the Lions' side, Slattery initiating a scalding blindside burst. Bennett had run a smart inside line and, rather than feeding those outside of him, as would have been the more natural thing to do, Slattery passed the ball to his left, not his right, and Bennett scored a try by deftly stepping inside of McCallum. The try was essentially conjured out of thin air, a piece of clever opportunism owing little to plans or tactics but everything to the ability to seize the moment.

The pièce de résistance, though, was sandwiched between the first and third tries. In a sense, fullback McCallum started the move by hacking the ball down the far-side touchline. In retrospect there is something slightly desperate to his initiative, a brave but misguided foray down a cul-de-sac with little help or understanding from his teammates. The Springbok fullback's improvisation ended with Bennett, deep inside his half, and, just like the famous try for the Barbarians against the All Blacks at Cardiff Arms Park six months before, Bennett skipped his way out of defence in a spirited counterattack before he was scragged by a brave Marais. But Bennett got his pass off just in time and the ball was relayed between the forwards (McBride–Brown–McBride) before the move collapsed like a spent wave on the beach. Uttley prodded the ball forward as it miraculously stayed inside the field of play and attempted to clumsily resuscitate the move. J.J. Williams joined him and, sensing the score, he also prodded the ball forward. As the try line loomed in his vision, Williams pounced on the favourable bounce as the cover defence was outstripped. It was a magnificent counterattacking move, the culmination not of planning per se, but of years of revolution and encouragement, a rugby culture in all its facets struggling to drag itself into a period in which it was suddenly physically, mentally and intellectually competitive with the giants of the south.

The Lions scored two more tries in the Test, both resulting from Springbok mistakes. For the fourth, McCallum failed to find touch after Bennett harried Bosch and the ball was shovelled to him in the hope that he could clear Bok lines as the home side played some catastrophically jittery rugby. Edwards gathered the McCallum kick and ran it back down the narrow side touchline unopposed, before slipping inside to Brown, who stormed over from close. To put too much emphasis on McCallum is possibly unfair because, not for the first time, the initial pressure had come from a Lions counter-shove and a wheeled scrum, with Du Plessis looping a one-handed basketball pass to Bosch in a desperate attempt to tidy up and have the ball cleared.

The fifth Lions try came from similarly pressured beginnings. Bayvel sent a terrible pass from the base of a lineout to Bosch, who fired a panic-stricken pass out to replacement centre Leon Vogel. Tied up by Lions defenders, the ball was prized from Vogel's grasp and Milliken sniped towards the corner flag, being helped over the try line by Ellis in a slightly mistimed tackle. Afterwards, five or six Boks milled around, hands on hips, at a loss for words. Watching the sequence today, it looks as if they are unable to grasp how Milliken had evaded all of their attentions. They look tired, confused, the *moer in*.

On the grandstand roof, Trevor Quirk was commentating for SABC radio and recalls noticing an increasingly disconsolate Gerhard Viviers alongside him. Quirk told me that the atmosphere for most of the game was almost funereal, until perhaps 'the last 10 or 12 minutes', when the crowd were shaken out of their disbelief and started to applaud the spectacle. 'He [Viviers] was close to me and he was so distraught he was almost suicidal. I thought there was a chance he was going to throw himself off the grandstand roof.' J.P.R. Williams was similarly touched by the atmosphere. He wrote in his autobiography that he would forever remember 'the image of the sun setting over the West stand, gradually shading more of the pitch, with the crowd growing quieter and quieter, as Loftus became a graveyard for South African rugby.'

Years later it is like watching a rabble or a retreating army. There is no order, no leadership and no plan. As the match progresses, the Lions sense this more and more strongly. Loftus becomes a canvas on which is told a story of abject surrender and humiliation. Not since the Springboks were beaten 20-3 in Wellington nine years previously have they suffered such a heavy defeat. They have not lost at Loftus for 27 years. Over the course of the hours to follow it suddenly dawns on the players, the rugby public and the administrators that the Springboks might lose their first series to the Lions this century. The day of reckoning will be at Boet Erasmus for the third Test in two weeks' time. In between, the tourists will fly on a chartered DC-3 to the southern section of the Kruger National Park for some boozy rest and relaxation. In the meantime, they repair to the post-match function, which is in a marquee erected on Loftus's B field. McBride, as is his wont, gives a charming, gracious speech. 'You'll forgive us,' he says to his audience, 'for whatever might happen later on, because Pretoria belongs to us tonight.'

6

A history of South African rugby photographs

MANY OF THE phrases dealing with introspection have an anatomical element, as though emotional discomfort is literally expressed – or voiced – through the human body. So we talk of 'hand-wringing' and 'teeth-gnashing'. We might even talk of 'navel-gazing' to denote a particularly acute form of introspection. The collective white psyche struggled to swallow the record Loftus defeat. It was not simply that the Springboks had leaked five tries, although that, of course, was part of it. There was also the manner of the defeat to consider – their emotional capitulation and the collapse of their spirit. The Boks were defensively disorganised; they lacked cohesion, playing as individuals rather than as a team. They lost two tightheads and were shaded in the lineouts; they lacked attacking thrust; they did not seem able to control the ball long enough in order to launch anything remotely ambitious. The list goes on and on.

Most damning of all was the fact that they were ultimately deserted by their courage. In our interview, Du Plessis shook his head gently when recalling the game. There was almost a puzzled look in his eyes, and although the bewilderment had softened over the years, he seemed unable to believe it when I told him the score of the match. 'Shit,' he said, 'that's a 40-pointer today,' which indicated to me that this was not a match he chose to revisit very often. Bravery is a touchstone of South African rugby. Springbok teams do not, as a rule, disintegrate, as, say, the French have a reputation for doing. In this Test, the Bokke did not rally or become marginally better. They were not improved by bench-strength or a raft of tactical substitutions 10 minutes into the second half. In fact, they became worse. They were subdued, toyed with and finally humiliated as they struggled to find touch and clear their lines, make tackles and keep some semblance of defensive shape. It was like being given a dose of old-fashioned Springbok medicine.

The embers of defeat were fanned with a kind of self-loathing glee by the Afrikaans press. The photograph on the front page of the following day's *Rapport* was quite remarkable. It showed Bennett in the foreground and McBride behind him, facing the camera. There is nothing untoward about this, except for the fact that McBride, who is watching Bennett and the mill of play in front of him, is smiling. His expression is one of utmost confidence, yet it also manages to be enigmatic, if only because rugby players do not smile. It is not part of the repertoire of acceptable rugby emotions. And smiling at someone on the rugby field suggests humiliation, and humiliation is the unacceptable face of defeat. Under the heading '*Hy lag mos vir ons*', he's laughing at us, is the following caption: '*Die man met die yslike glimlag op sy bakkies – dit, terwyl die wedstryd nog aan die gang is! – is Willie McBride, die Leeus se kaptein. Voor hom is Phil Bennett, een van die groot Leeu-helde van die wedstryd.*' (The man with the smile on his mug – and this while the match is still

going on! – is Lions captain Willie John McBride. In front of him is Phil Bennett, one of the big Lions heroes of the match.)

What upsets the caption writer is that McBride is smiling *while the game is still going on* – he has not even had the decency (or the politeness) to wait until the game is over. The subtext is that the Lions captain is so confident of victory that he is celebrating before the end because *he knows what the result will be.* In turn, this means that nothing the Springboks do will change the inevitable result, as if it were preordained. McBride knows this, as does his team. Time is standing still for the Boks and it is bending to the Lions' will, so much so that rugby etiquette can be dispensed with. McBride may as well make his post-match victory speech here and now. What advantage is to be gained from waiting?

There is much evidence to support the idea that the Lions

came to South Africa knowing they would win the series. There are two categories of McBride quotes from the tour, those leavened by the natural modesty that comes from being a visitor in another man's land, and those utterances that come from a moment of candour or happen unguarded and off the cuff. The latter are obviously the more trustworthy, such as McBride's famous 'You ain't seen nothing yet' quote from the bar of the Marine Hotel in Port Elizabeth after the third Test. They are not always confined to the captain. Sometimes Syd Millar hitched a ride on the candid-quote bandwagon. He predicted after the South Western Districts game in Mossel Bay, for instance, that the Lions would win the first Test, which is exactly what they did. In interviews both during and after the series, McBride was analytically vigilant, constantly on the lookout for the exact point where the match turned. In his interview after the first Test, he said he knew the match was won when the Springboks received a penalty and, rather than scrumming the Lions, opted for a lineout, which told him that they were running scared of his pack. In the third Test, at Boet Erasmus, McGeechan, of all people, cheekily snapped a drop goal between the uprights, opening up a decent lead after a tight first half. McBride forensically isolated this moment – not other, more obvious winning moments or passages of play – as the point at which the match (and so, of course, the series) was won. You get the idea, from all this evidence provided by McBride and his staff, that the man was simply casting about for instances to support what he already knew was going to happen. Having forged a theory, he was simply looking for illustrations to confirm it.

The McBride photograph in *Rapport*, with its distant Mona

Lisa echo, was merely a kind of front-page appetiser for the back-page feast to follow. Phil Zaayman's match report was headlined '*Sies, wat 'n Kafferpak*' (Sis, what a Kaffir-beating), further deriding the Boks' *vrot* performance with the idea that not only were they disgusting in defeat, but they had suffered a beating of the kind normally reserved for black people. The headline was the brainwave of Rykie van Rooyen, a pioneering Afrikaans journalist of the day and the newspaper's assistant editor. After doing a master's degree at Stellenbosch University in 1943/4, Van Rooyen went to work for *Die Burger* in 1945. It took her 30 years to work her way past the considerable obstacles placed before her by the patriarchs of the profession to a position of influence within the group's flagship Sunday newspaper. That said, her gender prevented her from becoming a parliamentary correspondent or part of the parliamentary team. Instead she was confined to writing a church column, doing book reviews and to sometimes writing hard news. There were clearly parts of the newspaper landscape that she was not allowed to probe.

According to Lizette Rabie, a media historian at Stellenbosch University who has written extensively about Van Rooyen, the headline was a way of winding up *Rapport*'s half-a-million readers. 'It was an expression of how they could do this, how they could play so dismally,' Rabie said, acknowledging that there was provocative intent on Van Rooyen's part. 'She wanted to stir. She understood the demography and psychography of her readership. She knew it would ruffle feathers and waited for the reaction. It came in the form of a bagful of letters the following week.'

Rabie said that Van Rooyen would have been disappointed to hear that many viewed the headline to be racist. She made the additional point that in condemning the headline, we are perhaps guilty of a kind of backward projection, finding it lacking according to the politically correct values of the present rather than the values of the time in which it was expressed. Van Rooyen was anything but racist, argued Rabie, and while she was frustrated at having constantly to bang her head against her profession's glass ceiling, hers was a gesture to be seen from within the codes of a particular constituency, something more inflammatory than anything else. Zaayman, however, was considerably more sentimental, bemoaning the performance in syrupy prose full of jingoism and unctuous paternalism. What seemed to perturb him most was that defeat had come at the hands of '*immigrante*', a group of red-shirted immigrants. As it was, the Springboks did not only lose, their 'pathetic play' was laughed at, derided. '*Om immigrante om jou kliphard te hoor lag vir ons Springbokke se patietiese spel was nie lekker nie.*' (To hear the deep laughter of immigrants at the Springboks' pathetic play is not pleasant.) So the once proud men in green were a bunch of jokers, receiving the kind of *klap* only meted out to black people. According to the terms of the headline, in losing the Test the Springboks had symbolically regressed to the level of those excluded from playing rugby for the national side. By losing to the degree and in the manner they had, they had lost their pride; in losing their pride they had lost the colour of their skin. J.P.R. Williams might have sensed a quietening of the fans' ardour as the shadows lengthened over Loftus. It was in other respects also the darkest of days.

The McBride photograph is not only significant for what it tells us about the Lions captain's self-knowledge. It is interesting because it forms part of the photographic history of

Springbok–Lions clashes, taking its place in a collection of photographs that tells more graphically and harrowingly the story of rugby between these foes than any newsreel footage or YouTube clips or ponderous histories ever could. The first photograph – and perhaps the most genteel of a rugby player ever – is that of Paul Roos at Richmond in 1906, taken by an unknown photographer. It shows a statuesque Roos standing alone in an empty field. In the middle-distance is a solid line of maple or chestnut trees, vague and slightly blurred in the gloaming. The photographer is kneeling or squatting, and so Roos looks larger than he should. The effect is one of a Springbok hero alone with his decency and courage, battling to establish the Springbok name. Roos's aloneness (this, I think, is the correct word, because Roos is not *lonely* per se, but there's an existential element to the photograph all the same) is accentuated by the shape of his shoulders and the heavy downward thrust of his legs. By modern standards he does not look muscular,

but mutely powerful in his long knickerbocker-type shorts and cumbersome boots. More than this, he looks trustworthy, morally powerful. He looks like someone who can be relied upon, which is presumably what you want from a Springbok captain. In a manner of speaking, it is exactly what you got in later captains like Craven, Claassen and Marais.

The second image in this threadbare canon is the famous Ivor Hanes photograph of Jack van der Schyff's aching miss of the conversion to Theuns Briers's try, a kick that would have given the Boks a one-point victory over the Lions at Ellis Park in 1955. In case we have forgotten, what makes this photograph so poignant is that Hanes has captured the exact moment when the ball skews past the upright; Van der Schyff, having already foreseen it, is trudging away from the place where he took the kick like a condemned man, his head lolling hopelessly on his chest. In the background, behind the posts, we see the Ellis Park scoreboard, which shows the British Isles' score on 23 points and the South Africans on 20-something. The '2' is present, filled in, but the next column is empty, awaiting the outcome of the kick. If the kick had been successful, a '4' would be rolled in, and the Springboks would have won the Test by one point. Van der Schyff's failed conversion, however, means that the Lions have won the Test 23-22.

The beauty and intrigue of Hanes's photograph is that the proverbial 'moment frozen in time' is revealed to be profoundly elongated, as it reaches back weakly into the immediate past of the match and strongly into the future. It is not simply a moment of good or bad fortune. I interviewed Hanes in August 2002 and remember him telling me that he had been at Ellis Park for a far more ordinary Currie Cup game between Transvaal and Western Province the previous weekend. Coming back

to the ground for the Test, Hanes again set himself up on the halfway line, with an unusual view of the scoreboard, which attracted much derision from the group of hardened press photographers covering the match. For some reason, he sensed the possibility inherent in the position of his camera, and indeed came away with the precious photograph he had doubtlessly been seeking, one of not only considerable aesthetic beauty and form, but also of narrative drama and emotion. 'I was always looking for something odd,' he said.

One of the reasons why the photograph has survived is that it is a formally robust image. It contains obvious verticals (the rugby posts and the players in the foreground), but is balanced by some equally strong horizontals in the shape of the stands surrounding the field, the markings on the field and the scoreboard itself. Within this network of verticals and horizontals, it also has a discernible tilt, in that the entire image gives the impression of collapsing slightly to the left as we see it. The ball, which is missing the uprights, 'swings' the photograph perceptibly to the left, as does Van der Schyff's demeanour, his collapsed head, as he walks dolefully across the frame from right to left. The photograph's leftward inclination is a prelude to something more absolute, because, in Van der Schyff's case, he literally slides – to coin a phrase – out of the frame. Ellis Park is the departure point for his ride down an increasingly slippery slope as, in time, he drifts out of Springbok rugby and slips out of the country. The photograph is a premonition, for in it we catch a glimpse of Van der Schyff's tragic future.

That Ellis Park Test in August 1955 was the first of four. After his missed conversion, Van der Schyff played no further part in the series, being dropped ahead of the second Test. He was made a scapegoat for the loss and never played for the Springboks again; he was literally excommunicated from the church of Springbok rugby. The use of the word 'scapegoat' is not unintentional, for in its strongest sense it means to be the bearer of the people's sins. Teams lose matches in many ways, and at many points throughout, so it is often no more than expedient to punish the kicker. He is the most obvious and transparent of the team's underachievers. By rights – and logic – he cannot be the only one, because if he is the only one his team should surely have won the game more comfortably.

The final irony in this sad story is that the man who replaced Van der Schyff at fullback in the second Test was a man that Hanes had seen the week before kicking for Western Province in the Currie Cup game at Ellis Park – Roy Dryburgh. In a sense, it was Dryburgh who inspired Hanes to return to his intriguing position on the halfway line, although Dryburgh's kick (another irony) had been successful and that photograph had none of the pain of Van der Schyff's. As history would have it, the second Test was at Newlands, Dryburgh's home ground. While not Van der Schyff's home ground, Newlands was the one venue in South Africa where he had been most comfortable and, as a result, most successful. One wonders how he would have fared there had he been given a second chance?

In time Van der Schyff emigrated, ultimately finding solace in the comparative anonymity of the Copper Belt, big-game hunting in Northern Rhodesia and playing a little bit of rugby on the side. It was a terrible way to be treated, but one wonders if Van der Schyff's own dejection, the collapsing of not only his head but his spirit, did not somehow sow the seeds of his own demise. It might inadvertently have been accelerated by Hanes's memorable photograph, where the difference between winning and losing is captured by a poignant square of emptiness on a scoreboard.

The third photograph in this brief montage is, like the Roos image, a subtle one. It has none of the pathos of the Van der Schyff photograph and none of the welling unfairness that makes a man who misses a kick ultimately responsible for defeat. The photograph is taken in 1962 and shows the two front-rankers, Fanie Kuhn and Syd Millar, walking towards the camera after the third Test between the Springboks and the Lions. The two men are fearsome and unsmiling, but, despite this, there is an unspoken bond between them, a respect borne of the fact that the two have wrestled against each other for the duration of the match and have come through their ordeal. Although Millar has survived, he is injured. You can see this by looking carefully at his left arm, which looks almost paralysed from the elbow down. It is not a crippling injury, yet Millar is holding the arm gingerly, as though he might have pinched

a nerve in his shoulder or tweaked something in his neck. In a sense it amounts to nothing more than a wartime injury. Here are two men, comrades in arms, walking off the field of battle. Above and beyond who has won, they have prospered in a deeper sense: they have survived. There is an unspoken camaraderie between the two warriors as they walk off side by side, and that is of a priceless experience shared.

It was memories of his encounters with men like Kuhn that coursed through Millar's rugby veins when he coached the Lions to South Africa 12 years later. His injunction to the team in Stilfontein when they arrived was that they should 'scrum, scrum and scrum some more'. It was a boring, tiresome mantra, but one borne of painful experience. Millar knew that the big set-piece engagements would be vital to the outcome of the series and set about choreographing the Lions pack to the point where they rolled into their opponents with a slick, frightening power. Watching them form up, bind together and walk into opposition packs as they bend down in unison is one of the most moving sequences of the tour. Shortly after the eight days at Stilfontein, Millar was quoted as saying he was unperturbed by the fact that the Lions had lost a couple of scrums on their put-in. It was not anything to be bothered about, he said, but it rarely, if ever, happened again. Millar and McBride, his first lieutenant, made absolutely sure of that.

If the Hanes photograph of Van der Schyff's agonising miss has a foretaste of the doom that was to follow the kicker as he dragged his curse through the wastes of Northern Rhodesia, so it is impossible not to see McBride's enigmatic smile in the 1974 photograph as a premonition of what was to follow. McBride was the smartest of men. He had reached maturity as a player and leader by the time '74 wound round. All the lessons and mistakes, all the amateur blather and the partying at the expense of winning, all the near misses, would be consigned to the past in South Africa. Roos could not smile in Richmond, for, as a pioneer, there was nothing to smile about; there was simply a future to face. McBride, by contrast, could afford to smile, for by the time of the second Test he could face the future with more equanimity and confidence than any captain of a Lions tour to South Africa before him.

*

After the Loftus debacle, Dugald MacDonald never again played for South Africa. He and Du Plessis overindulged at the post-match function and they had still more beers while waiting for their delayed flight down to Cape Town the following day.

It was confirmation of what the brains trust had long suspected: MacDonald was incorrigibly unconventional. The incident in which he threw his few clothes out of a hotel window on the Gazelles tour of Argentina was not isolated. Du Plessis would be redeemed by his pedigree and his connections, but MacDonald was banished, both literally and figuratively. It was many years before he spoke to Claassen again.

After his one and only Test in the green and gold, MacDonald went on to pursue a successful European rugby career. He played at Oxford University, spent two years at Toulouse and then went to Parma in Italy, where he fell in love with northern Italy and developed a fascination with Elvis Presley, Egyptology and the Torino football side's famous air disaster, which happened as they were returning from Portugal after a European Cup tie in 1949. Despite his many rugby achievements, as well as a successful life away from rugby (he owns several fruit farms in the Koue Bokkeveld), MacDonald remained a man with a thorn in his flesh. He told me in an interview that one always compiles lists of Springboks, grading them in ability from the finest to the most ordinary, a kind of parlour game, but one beloved of fans as much as players. He did not say it in so many words, but the intimation was that he was on such a list and he did not place himself anywhere near the top, although, under different circumstances, he might have made more of his bravery and talent. It was clear that he felt himself to be unworthy. 'The huge thing that used to dominate my mind was the second Test,' he told me over breakfast in Newlands in May 2013. 'You row by sitting backwards [MacDonald rowed single-handedly across the Atlantic in 2001] so you are always looking back into your past. I always felt myself to be hugely shameful and guilty about the loss at Loftus.'

In February 2013, three months prior to our interview, he was given the opportunity to deal with the feelings that had plagued him for nearly 40 years. MacDonald is the president of Ikeys rugby and helps out with coaching the first XV. The university was about to start its Varsity Cup campaign, and the Ikey Tigers travelled to Potchefstroom for a pre-competition friendly against North-West University's Pukke. He called Claassen and told him he was going to be in town, could they meet? MacDonald's former coach had no quibble and the two met up, despite the fact that MacDonald was 'absolutely shitting himself' and, as was the case all those years ago, was intimidated by the prospect of talking to the man. 'Claassen always used to ask, "*Is julle reg, manne*?" (Are you ready, men?),' MacDonald told me. 'He was a very formidable individual. You didn't really talk to him, or we didn't in those days. He epitomised the Springbok cause.'

The two talked for three hours. The conversation was raw and emotional. 'I told him that I'd never had the opportunity to say that I let him down, the jersey down and the country down,' MacDonald said, adding that Claassen was himself moved by the occasion, partly because he did not understand why MacDonald had not come to him sooner. 'He called the visit "a gift from God",' said MacDonald, which suggests that Claassen may have been haunted by some of his own demons when it came to the series. My interview with the former Springbok coach certainly suggested that this was the case. Without labouring the point, Claassen made it clear that he and his co-selectors had wanted to face the crisis and deal with it themselves. The best way to do that was to try to make things better. Despite the rafts of changes and the positional switches, the former coach and chief selector gave the impression that he acted throughout in good faith.

In replaying our conversation in my mind's eye, I have wondered whether Claassen considered resigning during the series, for he made much of not deserting his post. He certainly took considerable strain, because the side for the third Test was announced a full week after the second. While the Lions were off on a jolly, drinking beer and learning the difference between black and white rhino in the Kruger National Park, South African rugby was in mortal danger. The tourists were rapidly confirming the selectors' worst fears – that the men of the veld were being, in rugby terms at least, left behind.

7

There's a Lion on my stoep

ON THE MORNING after the second Test, the Lions climbed aboard a chartered Dakota and bumped from Wonderboom on the edge of Pretoria to Skukuza in the southern corner of the Kruger National Park. You can see them carrying plastic-wrapped trays of 24 Castle cans with them as they get off the plane and, although there was occasion to laze around the rest-camp pools (with shirts off, of course) and go on game drives, mostly they spent their time in a happy, beery stupor. 'It wasn't rest at all,' said J.J. Williams slightly hysterically many years later. 'It was four days of getting absolutely smashed.'

Falling under sociable J.P.R. Williams's spell, Billy Steele, the Scottish wing, found the going demanding. When he was not reading James Hadley Chase novels, scoring a quick 50 not-out in a scratch cricket game against the press on the Wanderers B field or sprinting 50 yards to deck Moaner van Heerden with a roundhouse right of fabled ferocity, J.P.R. was a legendary drinker. Having adopted Steele, the slightly surprising choice for the first two Tests, as a drinking buddy, he naturally expected him to keep up. While J.P.R., the definitive seventies man, had no difficulty in drinking all the time, Steele was not as battle-hardened. As one day segued alcoholically into the next, so Steele wilted. The pack looked on with a mixture of curiosity and trepidation as J.P.R. drank him under the table again and again. Lions' legend has it that Steele lost his place in the side for the third and fourth Tests because he never recovered from the many Castles of Kruger. 'J.P.R. was to blame,' said J.J. 'That's bloody true, actually.'

Fortunately, the official record paints a slightly more sober picture. Newsreel footage of the trip shows some of them packed into the back of pale-blue Toyota V8 pickups, gunning through the dust while rhino cows and their calves gambol within touching distance. There are African hornbills and red-bummed baboons, and elegantly lopsided giraffes sashaying through the veld like supermodels. Cameras are everywhere. The pack donned their aviator shades and got snapping with Instamatics and more sophisticated Japanese equipment. There is even footage of Davies, the Welsh number 8, dropping his camera in a small river. He gets his hand bitten by a baby crocodile as he tries to salvage it, to much hysterical laughter from his teammates.

The scribes trotted after all this like obedient ponies, struggling to find Skukuza's or Pretoriuskop's few available telephones so they could dictate chirpy colour stories ('Davies in croc shock!') to SAPA and the *Argus* in Johannesburg and Cape Town, or further afield to Fleet Street. One wonders what the *Daily Telegraph*'s John Reason, the most highbrow of the Brit press pack and a man who loathed the *Daily Mail*'s Terry O'Connor, made of the winter dust and the drab greenery. Game drives and walks were an acquired taste, as some footage of the desperately bored and uninterested Lions clearly shows. There were, after all, only so many times you could tell your wife about stumbling over a steenbok, as happened to Tom David, or soothing your insect-bitten legs with lamp oil, as was the case with many of the brood after one of their walks through the scrub and thorn bush. 'We'd hear so-and-so's down at the river, watching crocodiles, and so we'd rush off to get the story,' Shafto explained. 'In those days we dictated down the phone to a dictate-typist. Mrs Townsend was her name. She was brilliant – didn't miss a thing.'

Other than nursing niggles after the Test, the Lions were concerned about Bennett's injury. He had gashed his foot on the studs of Ian McCallum's boot in going round the Springbok fullback to score the Lions' second try and had wanted to go off. McBride pleaded with him to stay, telling him that Old's replacement, Gibson, had only just arrived and this was no time for the faint-hearted. By the end of the match Bennett was in considerable pain, and by the time the team arrived in Skukuza he was being piggybacked around because he did not want to put too much weight on the injury. After a boozy night around the campfire, he and McBride were making their way back to their rondavel when they heard the roar of a nearby lion. McBride panicked and started running through the darkness, shouting manically: 'It's every man for himself!' He did not see the overhanging tree branch until the last second. He ducked, but not quickly enough, and Bennett, who was on his back, got whacked on the head. Thankfully he was so drunk that he did not feel a thing and managed to hobble his way to safety. When the two awoke the next morning they noticed that their rondavel was on the edge of the camp, and so protected by the perimeter fence. A lion had made a kill just outside the camp and deposited the evidence before heading back into the bush.

Bennett was not much better off the following morning either, still nursing his gammy knee and his gashed foot. Both he and his skipper had sore heads – albeit for different reasons this time – but they were happy. The trip was more than half over. They were two up with two to play.

Wednesday morning saw the Lions return to Rand Airport in Germiston in the cumbersome Dakota to prepare for the following day's match against an Invitation XV called the Quaggas. There had been speculation in the press that the powers-that-be might take the opportunity to draft some talented black players into the invitation side – a Morgan Cushe, say, or an Errol Tobias, perhaps even a Turkey Shields – to see whether they had rugby's equivalent of the right stuff. Piet Koornhof stonewalled unhelpfully, responding to queries by saying speculation was unwarranted, shorthand for the fact that neither the government nor the board had the slightest intention of having a black Quagga. For what it was worth, Koornhof's position on mixed sport (and mixed teams) was nothing if not splendidly incoherent. At much the same time as the Quaggas match, he was asked by *Rand Daily Mail*'s Trevor Bisseker how he felt about the Aurora Cricket Club in Pietermaritzburg continuing to field a mixed team in their local cricket league. Koornhof's answer is a masterpiece of the genre: 'That is very wrong of them [Aurora]. For them to continue playing like this is not in the interests of non-White players or the White players in the team, because if they continue to flout the acknowledged value systems of the country, and if that were to happen in all sport types, then I foresee sport chaos ensuing in the country. I have repeatedly asked them not to proceed with it, and I invite them to come and see me before the new season starts.'

As it was, the Quaggas side was made up of some of the country's most promising young players and those considered unlucky to have somehow slipped through the net, either in playing only a limited role in the trials or in having been neglected altogether. Such players included Johan 'Klippies' Kritzinger, the Transvaal utility forward, who was shifted to eighthman on the eve of the match to make way for Natal's Binkie Kapp, who had replaced Rhodesia's Brian Murphy at lock, and South Eastern Transvaal's livewire loose forward, Polla Fourie. In the backs, there was curiosity about the happening Eastern Province centre, Gavin Cowley, as well as the talented young Western Province under-20 flyhalf and promising cricketer, Peter Kirsten.

An Ellis Park crowd can never be described as genteel. Fifty thousand people (including two national selectors, Claassen and Daan Swiegers) packed into the old hulk of a stadium on Thursday afternoon to watch a friendly of no great significance ahead of the far more important match against Orange Free State the coming Saturday. Even though the ban on naartjies had been lifted – punters brought vast quantities of them, as well as oranges and cans, into the ground – a crowd of this size for a midweek match is remarkable. This is partly explained by the fact that the fans, like the selectors and the rugby-loving population at large, were becoming increasingly entranced by the Lions. They were also looking for a performance to soothe the bruises and lacerations of Loftus, as well as casting about for the method to unlock the Lions' secret. By now the selectors were so desperate that they were willing to grab onto anything significant that might help in their team selection prior to the next Test. Certainly the Quaggas had talent in their midst, just enough for the faithful to hope that the hoodoo would be broken. Fourie was a barrelling loosie in the Ellis mould; Cronje was returning from his shoulder injury; and then there was Kirsten, slight and nimble, but with a fine pair of hands.

The naartjie-eaters were not disappointed. Kirsten pocketed three penalties for the Quaggas and also succeeded with a drop kick from a full 55 metres out. 'It was one of the finest drop goals seen at Ellis Park for a long time, and came after the Lions had been penalised just inside their own half, close to the touchline,' wrote a group of *Rand Daily Mail* staff reporters for the newspaper's front page the following day. 'Kirsten elected to drop instead of place the ball and it sailed high and true through the uprights.'

With Kirsten in fine fettle at 10, the Quaggas also scored a try through Border winger Alan Stephenson to give them 16 points. But it was not quite enough. The Lions scored 20 points, through tries to Brown (two) and Ripley, and two penalties and a successful conversion by Irvine.

As the second half progressed, the large crowd became increasingly vocal in their objections to the refereeing of Natal's Ian Gourlay. They had lugged an unstable compound of frustration and post-Loftus disappointment to the ground, and some of Gourlay's decisions seemed frankly ridiculous. Brown's first try was awarded despite the lock appearing to not ground the ball, and the local press spotted what they thought were two knock-ons in the move that led to the Scot's second try. Gourlay did not seem to extend the same kind of privileges to the home side. He was pedantic on what he deemed to be a marginal forward pass from Cronje to Cowley as the centre hared downfield. By the time Gourlay blew the final whistle, the crowd, never the most warm-hearted or forgiving of folk anyway, was enraged. As he left the field, many of those naartjies that had not been nibbled at nervously as the Quaggas tried to reel in the lead, rained down. So did oranges, even cans. A spectator tackled Gourlay as fans stormed the field. Brown, possibly feeling that he needed to intervene on Gourlay's behalf after the referee's generosity, came to his rescue, as did a group of policemen who had been watching proceedings from the side of the field. It was not, however, before someone had managed to get in a kick and a punch as Gourlay lay on the ground.

Although the referee was quoted in the press as saying he was not bothered by the fracas, the *Rand Daily Mail* cast aside their usual snotty caution and experienced a tabloid moment. 'Ellis Park erupted in riot yesterday as thousands of spectators stormed onto the field after the Lions had beaten the Quaggas 20-16 and started assaulting referee Ian Gourlay,' their team of staff reporters wrote. 'Police were caught flat-footed as Mr. Gourlay was brought down from behind by a white-shirted spectator, who fell on top of him and punched him as he lay on the ground. Other spectators then joined in the fray, hitting and kicking at the referee as touch judge Cas de Bruyn – and some Lions, led by Gordon Brown – rushed to help. There had been warnings of spectator unrest earlier in the game, with some of Gourlay's decisions bringing boos and naartjies from spectators packing the popular side of the ground.'

It is highly unlikely that thousands stormed onto the field, even though the natives on 'the popular side of the ground' were unnaturally restless. Tickets on the eastern side of Ellis Park were cheaper than elsewhere, although the annoyance with Gourlay and the frustration with the Quaggas for titillating them were not confined to those in the cheaper seats. More significant than the *Rand Daily Mail* going to town on the numbers was the fact that the tourists were now under South Africa's skin. To some extent, they understood this. They read the newspapers and had a sophisticated handle on public opinion. The city of Springbok rugby was not quite sacked and crumbling, but the flags were not flying at full mast. Claassen and his representatives were everywhere, which meant that while they were giving a plausible impression of doing their job, they also did not have the slightest idea of where some of their next team was going to come from. In a word, they were panicking. The Lions' next match, against a strong Orange Free State, would prove to be clarifying – in ways that had probably not been envisaged.

The Lions only flew down to Bloemfontein on the Friday afternoon, so they returned to the venue of the Quaggas game the following day, practising in the Johannesburg sun at Ellis Park in the morning. The journalists were there in the empty ground to witness Edwards doing a fair bit of kicking from the base of the scrum; a way, the scribes realised, to compensate for the fact that McGeechan, the likely flyhalf against Free State, only had one reliable foot – his left. They also noticed J.P.R. Williams frequently joining the line in rehearsed moves, which led them to believe that they would probably witness a game as open as the veld they were about to fly across. It was not to turn out that way at all.

Lions management had dubbed the match against Orange Free State a 'prestige fixture' and the visitors were well aware of the Free Staters' *bona fides*. Choet Visser had for a long time talked up what he considered to be his team's prospects, and they were one of the form domestic sides of the period. Not only had they been the losing Currie Cup finalists of the previous season, but two weeks prior to the Lions fixture they had narrowly lost to the Junior Springboks, effectively a shadow Springbok side, by a meagre four points late in the game. In addition, they had a number of players who were there or thereabouts when it came to possible Springbok selection: Johan de Bruyn (lock), Rampie Stander (tighthead prop), Kleintjie Grobler (eighthman), Gerrie Sonnekus (scrumhalf) and Jan Schlebusch (centre) all knew that one good game could catapult them into the squad for the third Test two weeks hence. The rumour mill was freighted with some very heavy traffic at the time (there was a discussion in the Afrikaans daily press, for example, about Gerald Bosch reverting to fullback for the third Test to make way for the more rounded Jackie Snyman at flyhalf) and South African rugby was spinning on its axis far more quickly than the mandarins were comfortable with or would usually allow. The Free Staters were a proud lot, keen for their players to not only step into the garden of the Springbok elect, but also to demonstrate that the sport demanded to be played openly and attractively. Rugby had a moral imperative, and this involved playing with brio and flair, if at all possible. It was all stacking up rather nicely.

Despite what we must accept as the teams' best intentions, it did not quite run that way, with scoring in Saturday's quietly violent match kept to a minimum. Indeed, there were only two tries in the entire game, both of them to the Lions, both of them towards the end of a half or, in the case of their second, in injury time, as the contest seemed all but won by Orange Free State. The first came from the scragging of Sonnekus close to his line. A maul was formed and the ball (not for the first time on tour) came out on the Lions' side when it might have been expected to do otherwise. Davies barged round the blindside and dived over pretty much on the halftime whistle to give the Lions a one-point lead (3-4) after Snyman's earlier penalty. The score was no straightforward affair. Some felt Fergus Slattery had impeded Harold Verster, the Orange Free State flank, as Verster flew towards Davies. After nearly 40 years, Germishuys certainly knows how he sees it: 'The try they scored – there was a blindside move and Slattery pulled Harold, our flanker, back. The touch judges and referees didn't see that. They did see it when somehow Kleintjie Grobler's try was disallowed after he went over.'

The theme established in the first half continued in the second. It was a tight, even brutal, affair, punctuated by the odd sniping break by both teams. For the home side, Germishuys had a strong run on the left wing, the move almost being completed with a try by Schlebusch, and Pikkie du Toit, the Free State centre, burst through without being able to round off, as his team inched ahead through a Snyman drop kick and a second penalty. Just when it seemed as though the Free Staters would sneak it with a two-point cushion (9-7), so the Welsh trio of Davies, Edwards and J.J. Williams pulled a fiendish trick from their collective sleeve.

Davies explained afterwards that he had noticed that, unlike in Wales, South African grounds tended to have clocks (sponsored by Lexington in this case) on their scoreboards. Looking up at the clock he realised that time was running out for the Lions and he had a quick word with Windsor. They were in striking distance of the Orange Free State line, and although

Sonnekus was feeding in to a reduced pack (lock Stoffel Botha was receiving treatment for an injury off the field), Windsor simply *had* to strike if the match was to be salvaged. This he did, and the ball was funnelled through the Lions forwards; Edwards, knowing he had precious little time, sniped blind. As he did so, he heard the unmistakable voice of his Welsh teammate, J.J. Williams, shouting 'Ga, Ga, Ga, give it to me' inside of him. As he was tackled achingly short of the line, he flung the ball inside; Williams gobbled the pass and dived over for a moment of pure satisfaction.

It was a remarkable score in a match of incredible physical intensity, Lions manager Alun Thomas admitting afterwards that his team probably did not deserve their victory. 'In certain respects we were pretty lucky,' he confessed after his team's 11-9 win. Millar, as was his wont, was more technical. He made the point post-match that the Free State pack had been very impressive, and that the Lions had been unable to dictate matters from the tight phases as they had done so often before on the tour. By now the selection panel was prepared to clutch at any straw. The two decent performances by South African opposition – the headline on Le Roux's match report in *Volksblad* said '*Vrystaters wys Bokke hoe om in te klim*' (Free Staters show Boks how to climb in) – after the Loftus debacle suddenly attained a status they possibly did not deserve. There was only one more match of any import before the Springbok team for the third Test would be announced, and that was against Northern Transvaal in a week's time. The side would be weighted heavily with those who did well against the Lions in the matches after the second Test.

Although neither set of players had any fundamental beef

with the snarling brutality of the Free State match, in retrospect the fixture had a less savoury dimension. This had to do with the Lions' maturing aptitude for gamesmanship and the feeling at large in Orange Free State rugby circles that Edwards had wound referee Gert Bezuidenhout round his little finger. This might be nothing more than a well-developed sense of sour grapes, although Piet van Zyl, one of three potential fullback candidates along with Frikkie Naudé and Gysie Pienaar going into the match, has no doubts at all about what transpired. Bezuidenhout, he said, 'pleaded' with both teams not to fight after the disputed first try, as he put forward the argument that Free State's best chance of victory was tied up with the pack remaining self-controlled. 'He told us that we were playing so well, and if we started fighting we might lose the match,' remembered Van Zyl. 'Unfortunately the try [to Davies] stood and that was his way of trying to calm us all down.'

Two weeks prior to the Lions game, Pienaar had made his debut in Orange Free State's 22-24 loss to Transvaal, and, with Van Zyl's ankle injury slow to heal and Naudé being second choice, the likelihood was that Pienaar's rangy counterattacking would hold sway against the Lions. As it happened, Pienaar did not play because he fell ill before the game, being hospitalised with bronchitis. This created a space for Van Zyl, who remembers the weeks before and the match itself with peerless clarity. 'Lots of punches were thrown in the scrums,' he said, recalling hooker Bestbier's black eye and the fact that some Free State forwards needed stitches afterwards. Listening to him carefully suggests that he is prepared to condone all of this; indeed, he sees it as part and parcel of the sport. What he takes issue with is Edwards's urbane manipulation of the officials. 'A few minutes – two or three at the most – from the end we were leading 9-7 and were awarded a scrum,' he recalled of the incident that led to the Williams try. 'Our lock, Stoffel Botha, had picked up a head injury in the move leading up to that scrum. As he received treatment it was recommended that we bring on our replacement forward, Wilhelm Potgieter. As the scrum was formed, Edwards complained to Mr Bezuidenhout that Potgieter was "illegally" on the field, as he did not have a doctor's note. [In those days the replacements had to bring a doctor's note from the sideline doctor to the referee.] On that technical issue Potgieter was sent off and we were stuck with seven forwards. At the time I think we thought we could hold our own, but that is history now. The Lions won the only tight head of the match as Edwards broke blind and J.J. Williams scored the winning try. It broke 45 000 supporters' hearts.'

The match aside, the weekend in Bloemfontein is also remembered for the hosts' incredible hospitality. The local Vintage Car Association was on hand to meet the Lions when they touched down at J.B.M. Hertzog International Airport and the cavalcade into town was long and happy, full of gently spluttering old bangers with Lions in them, waving regally to passers-by. 'It was like a royal wedding,' commented Nico du Plessis, Choet Visser's grandson, who had pride of place sitting alongside reserve hooker Ken Kennedy in one of the cars. 'Hundreds of people were there on the airport balcony and many of them were lining the road from the airport, a route of about 20 kilometres. They came out in their thousands.' With the Lions in his backyard, Visser was understandably in his element. Before the match a select group of them had wandered over to his inner-city carpet shop and ventured into his wife Joyce's florist shop next door. They sipped tea, larked about and posed for photographs. McBride rolled out his old gag to the effect that there were no oranges in the province that he could see, that it was not free and it was in one helluva state. His teammates rolled their eyes and smiled wanly.

The post-match function was at the Clarendon Hall, which for the home side was more a battlefield dressing station than a reception venue. The Free Staters arrived bloodied and bruised, still smarting from their last-minute defeat. Bestbier's eye was 'blue, swollen and almost closed', while Botha, who did not make it back onto the field, was covered in pieces of plaster. 'Blood was still dripping from captain Jake Swart's gashed eyebrow when he went up to make his after-match speech,' reported SAPA's Neil Cameron.

Despite struggling with his gash, Swart was magnanimous in defeat. The atmosphere at the function was cordial, with the match being left where it belonged. As he said his thank-yous and paid his respects, Swart joked that the Lions had won the match and if a beauty contest were to be arranged then and there, they would undoubtedly win that too. The guests laughed as the joke helped to further reduce any lingering tensions.

When the speeches were over, the Lions presented Visser with a plaque and Joyce was given not a box of Quality Street chocolates, bubble bath or luxury soap as may have been expected under the circumstances, but a mantle clock. The pièce de résistance, however, was yet to come. It came in the form of a wooden Welsh love spoon, a strangely tribal offering in this most secular of gatherings. One can only imagine the private conversation between the Vissers about what to do with the love spoon and where to put it, although Choet would have found out soon enough that it had no practical function. Welsh love spoons date back to possibly the 17th century. They are often carved with symbols of love and Celtic crosses, and are meant to signify romantic intent. In Visser's case there was in all likelihood a slight in-joke; he was missing his missus and the Lions were probably having a little good-natured fun at his expense.

Sunday evening was spent at Visser's private residence. The occasion was the formal opening of his rugby museum, and he invited the Lions and a select group of friends round for a braai and a singalong with an Argentine guitarist called Peter Kember, otherwise known as 'Chaco' to his friends. As a hard-tackling flank, Kember had turned out for a midweek Argentine selection against McBride when the Irish toured in 1971 and he had a strong feeling for their worth as players. Kember's father, Eric, sat on the Orange Free State Rugby Union board, and it was through him that Visser had contacted Peter in Buenos Aires with a view to having a *jol* in South Africa. 'I wasn't doing much at the time because of knee ligament damage,' Kember told me. 'In those days you were sometimes worse off when they operated, so I sold what I had, my car and a few bits and pieces, and caught a plane to Joburg. I arrived just before the Quaggas game and followed the rest of the tour. Choet wanted me to play Spanish guitar and sing songs – 'La Bamba' and 'Guantanamera' – to the Lions as part of the opening. It was a festive night, all of us packed into that small space.'

After a couple of speeches, Kember played his repertoire of happy and not-so-happy songs, and they consumed long and hard – indeed, the Lions ate like wolves. 'They kept on coming into the kitchen to ask for more potatoes,' recalled Visser's daughter. 'That was a problem because we hadn't served any of the other guests. We didn't want to refuse – a hostess can never refuse – so it took a long time for everyone else to get served.' Despite technical hitches in the kitchen, it was a memorable evening. Visser's museum, on garage level in his two-storey orange-brick house in a Bloem suburb, was full of artefacts and memorabilia, including photographs of Visser with that well-known rugby couple Liz Taylor and Richard Burton, his boxing friends and other members of the international glitterati. Still, no one quibbled. This was Visser's big day, and nobody was going to haggle too much over criteria. McBride loved South African food, their folksy ways and family life, as did the *sterk manne* of the team, McLauchlan, Windsor and Millar. There was another aspect of *die saai lewe* to which McBride responded warmly. When I asked someone why he appeared to enjoy South Africa so much more than New Zealand, a country that was similar in so many ways, they said that the clincher was that the South African women were so much more convivial and attractive.

The next item on the Lions' tick-list was a midweek fixture against Griqualand West in Kimberley. On a field almost entirely devoid of grass, the redshirts casually ran in 12 tries (Tom Grace grabbing four of them, Billy Steele getting two) in a match that was more of a training run than a gallop. Like so often on tour against this standard of opposition, the Lions prospered after halftime, scoring more points than there were minutes in the half in amassing 44 points to end 69-16 winners. Nelie Smith, the Bloem-based national selector, was on hand to witness it all. He kept a particularly watchful eye on the Griquas scrumhalf, Gert Schutte, who had briefly replaced

Bayvel in the second half of the match between the Quaggas and the Lions the previous week. Schutte, who was a Springbok reserve for the one-off Test against England in '72, was there or thereabout in the selectors' reckoning, and so needed to be monitored. Bayvel, the second-Test scrumhalf, was unlikely to retain his place and a player like Dirk de Vos, the Northern Transvaal scrumhalf, had so lost confidence that he had been dropped by his province and did not, in fact, play against the Lions at all. In the event, Schutte's big chance did not materialise, as the selectors made their most controversial decision of the tour in choosing the Orange Free State's Sonnekus, nominally an eighthman, at scrumhalf for the third Test.

By waltzing in 12 tries against Griquas, the Lions were squarely in what might be dubbed their rococo or High Mannerist phase, the most fancy and exuberant flowering of their talent. The Griquas game was their 15th, and after it they had rampaged to 78 tries in all, a handy average of over five tries per match. Even excepting the high-scoring provincial games against the *volstruisboere* and the *mielieboere*, the Lions easily passed the '68 Lions' total of 55 tries in 20 matches. And contrast McBride's team's 78 tries at this stage of the tour, for example, with the 13 tries against, seven of which had happened early, as the Lions had conceded two against Western Transvaal, two against South West Africa and three against Eastern Province. Since their sixth match on tour, against Western Province, where they conceded two, their opponents had only scored four tries against them, with one apiece to Southern Universities and the Quaggas, and two to Griquas themselves. Backline players such as J.J. Williams were among those with the highest tally, but forwards like Brown and, latterly, Davies, were scoring at decisive times in important matches. It was worrying for the scribes, the men who rolled and diligently shaped the dough of public opinion. Those more historically inclined pointed out that the last try scored by a Bok was Peter Cronje's against France in Durban in 1971, the second match in a brief two-Test series. That was a full three Tests ago, and far too much time had passed since. While the South African economy thundered along with one of the highest growth rates in the world and the Oriental Plaza opened amid some controversy in Fordsburg on the western side of the Johannesburg CBD, Israeli Uri Geller could be heard on SABC radio encouraging housewives to indulge in a risqué spot of teaspoon-bending before their hubby came home from work. If only the Boks could bend one of those Super Springboks across the line themselves, maybe life would begin to take on a slightly different flavour.

The following day the Lions squad repaired to a local farm to hunt. It was an occasion the headline writers found irresistible, because the quarry was springbok. All in all, 17 of the buck were shot, Tony Neary proving to be the best marksman. While not everyone participated, the symbolism was abundantly clear. Whether scoring tries against them or shooting them, the Lions continued to do pretty much as they pleased with the springboks. The tour was now more than half over, and only one game of significance in pure rugby terms other than Tests three and four remained, and that was against Northern Transvaal in four days' time.

As the province with probably the greatest reserves of player strength in the country, given that it drew some of its provincial and club players from the army bases on the outskirts of Pretoria, Northern Transvaal was expected to run the Lions as close as Orange Free State had, although there were lingering questions about the speed and thrust of its backline. It is not far-fetched to say that the Currie Cup champions took their collective personality from the complexion of the city itself: it was a martial side, one of unbridled state and Afrikaner power. Seven of the starting line-up against the Lions were from Police (Luther, Kidson, Jacobs, Booysen, Van Heerden, Eloff and Oosthuizen); one (Piston van Wyk) was from Weermag, as the Army rugby club was called; and Aucamp, the winger, came from Prisons. It would have been interesting if, for the sake of variation, a long-haired arts graduate or bohemian from Tukkies or Adelaar was included in the side, the Northerns equivalent of, say, Andy Ripley, with his cheesecloth shirts and flagrant bohemian ways. But this was not the case. Northerns were a power side, piano movers rather than piano players, to adapt an old French adage.

Despite their self-evident strengths, their short-term form was poor. They had drawn with South West Africa in Windhoek the previous weekend and, on the weekend prior to that, had lost in a friendly to Natal. Consequently, the fans stayed away, John Reason commenting that he had never seen a city as quiet as Pretoria was before the game. Unlike the Test two weeks earlier, there were vacant sections in the stadium, which was unusual. The punters simply did not have the bounteous faith of those who had watched Orange Free State or, for that matter, the 50 000 who had dragged themselves (and their naartjies) to the Thursday afternoon game against the Quaggas at Ellis Park in the hope that Kirsten and Fourie would bend the match in their direction.

With collective confidence in short supply in the lead-up

to the match, De Vos was not the only player wrestling the demons of form. The Northerns selectors for the Lions game dropped him and six others, with players like Tonie Roux, Louis Moolman and Wynand Claassen being left out. Butch van Wyk, son of At, an old Griquas and *mielieboer* stager, replaced De Vos at scrumhalf, and Roux lost his place to Luther at fullback. Other than Bennett, who still had not recovered from his foot injury, the Northerns' opponents were at full strength. McGeechan played in the Bennett berth, which meant that Gibson filled the McGeechan vacancy alongside Milliken in the centre; Andy Irvine played in Steele's place on the wing, a herald for what would come to pass at Boet Erasmus; and, as far as the forwards were concerned, Slattery was rested at flank, the quicksilver Neary taking his place. These changes were either pragmatic or cosmetic, and were not likely to be overly disruptive, with McGeechan growing in confidence in his new-found role. Edwards was on hand to help him with tactical kicking, and the front row and locks were the strongest possible combination. Davies, so important in the Free State match, was about to play another clever, inspirational game from the back of the scrum.

The pre-match predictions were spot on. Although Northern Transvaal's strength at forward kept them in the game, they had neither the adventure nor the brio of the Orange Free State backs and had to be content with banging over penalties through Luther. With the Lions cleverly staying away from Northerns lock Williams by throwing to Davies at the back of the lineout, they were able to control the pace of the game. Shortly before halftime Davies scored from close, his fellow loose forward, Neary, popping up in the second half to do exactly the same.

Despite their two tries, the Lions only carried a one-point lead deep into the second half. With the score at 13-12 in favour of the visitors, Luther, having succeeded with four penalties already, stepped up to take what pundits believed was going to be the defining kick. It was only 30 metres out and looked relatively straightforward, but Luther slid it wide and, with Irvine's final penalty being successful, the Lions ran out deserved 16-12 winners. This was not Norman Canale's view, and the *Sunday Times* correspondent saw nothing wrong with testing his readers' credulity. 'No team likes to go back and the Lions were no exception,' Canale wrote in the following day's newspaper. 'They went back plenty yesterday and suddenly the mantle of greatness didn't fit quite so immaculately on the sturdy shoulders of Gareth Edwards, the world's best scrumhalf.'

*

In the winter of 1973, the Netherlands, London Counties and Italy had visited South Africa. The Italians played teams like Rhodesia, Natal and Western Transvaal, and although their tour was less than successful in terms of results, there was occasion for quiet optimism, even unintended humour. In a report submitted to the Italian Federation that has found its way into the SARB archives, the Italians' manager, Giuseppe Alessandra, commented: 'Our first eight men have always been superior to their very strong opponents, always fighting with courage and intelligence. The South Africans were struck by – even envious of – the extraordinary strong scrum which seemed to be made up of dwarves (especially the front rank).' Brian Streak, writing for the *Sunday Mail* after Rhodesia's 42-4 victory over Italy in June 1973, managed to neatly sidestep the vagaries of translation to point out that while the Italians were callow, there was talent in their midst. 'The highest praise,' reported Streak, 'that can be handed to the Italian rugby team is their ability to handle the ball like magicians. The kindest thing that can be said of this "baby" of the International Rugby Board competition – they try.'

With a successful bridge having been built – a sort of rugby Ponte Vecchio – between the federations, the SA Africans, otherwise known as the Leopards or the African XV, responded positively the following year to an invitation from the Italian Federation for a six-match tour at the beginning of the South African season. The trip was generously underwritten by Stellenbosch Farmers' Winery and ended up being memorable for the players, most, if not all, of whom were travelling overseas for the first time. Morgan Cushe and Peter Swartz, flanker and flyhalf respectively in the squad to Italy, remember the dizzy mixture of trepidation and excitement as they struggled to familiarise themselves with anything Italian while they fretted away their final weeks in the semi-rural Eastern Province. 'There was this guy called Julio Govone,' Swartz told me from his humble home in Rosedale, a suburb of Uitenhage, in the winter of 2013. 'He was an Italian engineer and he worked out here for the Uitenhage municipality. He lent us a couple of books, just so we could get used to some Italian phrases. We learnt to say *bene*, *buongiorno* and *come sta*, so at least we knew some words in the language.'

The tour was not without its controversies, however. Shortly before the team was due to depart, their administrative number was swelled with the addition of a white Xhosa-speaking bureaucrat called Louis Koch. Administrators in the South

African African Rugby Board were perturbed, rightly sensing that Koch, who worked as chief director of the Cape Midlands Bantu Affairs Administration Board, was a government appointee and had been parachuted in to keep an eye on them. The Proteas tour of England in 1972 had contained several incidents of misbehaviour and, according to Ray ka Msengana, writing in the *Cape Times* before the Leopards departed, the government's precautionary step of appointing Koch arose 'after rumours that all was not well on the Proteas tour of the United Kingdom two years ago'. Quite what the Proteas' alleged misbehaviour had to do with the Leopards nobody knows, although clearly 'the *Bantoes*', as they were referred to in some SARB correspondence of the time, were not to be entirely trusted. As it happened, Koch's appointment and the response to it was probably more symptomatic of the exaggerated pride and mistrust that dominated rugby relationships across the colour line, because he did not, in fact, replace manager Nelson Mabuna as was originally thought. Both accompanied the side to Italy in May and, with coach Alfred Dwesi, ensured that it was a memorable tour.

Of more import than the Koch brouhaha (he was possibly also there to safeguard some of the sponsors' interests) was the fact that on the eve of the Leopards' flight to Rome, the team captain, Harry Ketelo, injured his wrist. This caused immediate disquiet, because Ketelo was outspoken and some felt the injury would be used as an excuse to leave him behind. He had complained about conditions at one of the team's pre-tour camps and did not like the way players were being addressed by certain officials. Despite insisting that he would be able to play with the support of a wrist guard, Ketelo was indeed left behind. He was replaced by the more pliable Liston Ntshongwana, who led the team out under floodlights against Lazio in Rome in their first match. The contest was a tight affair, with the Leopards' points coming from 'a Gareth Edwards–type break' by scrum-half Gibson Gawulayo, who passed the ball to winger Toto Tsotsobe to dot down. Although Vusumzi Nakani crossed Lazio's line for a late try, the score was disallowed and Lazio ran out 6-4 winners. It was to be the start of the Leopards' suspicions about dodgy refereeing.

Tsotsobe scored his second try of the trip in the Leopards' 16-all draw with the Italian under-23s in the third game of the tour in Parabiago, and his third in the final game of the sojourn against a Selection XV called the Dogi in Padua, a game the Leopards narrowly lost 9-14.

By far the most important game of the trip, and one that was afforded Test status by the Italian Federation, was the fifth, against Italy in Brescia. The Leopards managed to keep in touch until halftime, Cushe scoring a 22nd-minute try (converted by Swartz) and Charles Mgweba, the left wing, scoring a second on the cusp of halftime. Unfortunately Italy's superior scrummaging finally won the day against the lightweight black romantics of the Cape. 'Our rugby was strong but not so much,' said Cushe. 'We always believed in running it, not like the whites. The whole idea was because we were very light we must use speed and handling skills and support play. Those were the main things.'

With the greatest will in the world, the Leopards could not prosper playing such a naive, free-flowing game. Their most convincing result was the one they achieved against the Italy under-23s, with all the other matches being narrowly lost with the exception of the Test, where they were beaten 25-10. There were compensations, however, some headier than others. They got to see Italy's easy beauty, the gorgeous girls and the old men nursing espressos while lazily filling out their *totocalcio* coupons in sidewalk cafés. Facing the Dogi and the Zebre, the two invitation sides, they even got to play against players like Nelson Babrow, the son of Springbok Louis Babrow, as well as the New Zealander Jock Turner.

The Leopards discussed the game with the privateers and took tips, soaking up the priceless joy of being away from apartheid South Africa. They learnt to enjoy the company of their trustworthy bus driver, complained again about the standard of Italian refereeing and jealously guarded their daily allowance. Cushe went shopping and fell in love with a chequered sports jacket that he was unable to ask the price of because his Italian was so rudimentary. He had to ask the team's bus driver to act as interpreter and eventually the deal was sealed. Despite Koch's efforts at being the perfect chaperone, he could not keep an eye on everyone, and one or two Leopards behaved like Proteas, or, for that matter, Springboks. 'Next to our hotel in Rome,' remembered Swartz, 'was a legalised brothel for those with low morals. So one of us – a very naughty one – pops across there. After he has done his thing we see him running fast down the street, very fast. He was going to be shot because he didn't want to pay.'

Other than their exposure to a more decent and civilised world, Cushe, Mgweba and Tsotsobe left Italy as better rugby players. Cushe was an interesting case. A galvanic, smart flank who had heart, guile and, lust for glory, he was born Eric but nicknamed Morgan by his father, Simon, who had been mesmerised by Cliff Morgan when the Lions toured South Africa in 1955. Originally a handy junior middleweight, rugby at first held little charm for Cushe. 'I was not impressed with rugby,' he said with a sniff, until he was knocked down in the ring and sensibly decided to pursue other sporting options. He was not big, but he had decent hands and got around. Flyhalf or fullback suggested themselves as natural positions. 'I looked around at Swallows – and there were two Springbok centres there – and I said to myself no, no, no, it would take me years to be a centre,' he told me. 'I looked around again. I saw two old flanks, good but going down, so the coach said it was a good idea for me to become a flank.'

Cushe found it difficult to leave boxing behind. He became involved in undercard bouts on the side of the scrum, or lingered, throwing crisp punches, while the game moved off elsewhere. He needed to be taken in hand. Coach Doug Kopo explained to him that he could not retaliate for every late tackle or perceived infringement. Swallows were conceding penalties and leaking points; Cushe had to keep his temper under control. The message seemed to get through, because Swallows were Eastern Province champions in '68, '70 and '71. Cushe formed a fine partnership with his older brother Meshak, nicknamed Stampo after a popular cartoon character of the day, and began to earn a deserved reputation as not only a rugby player, but also a rugby thinker. By the time the Lions trampled towards Mdantsane outside of East London in July 1974, he was in something like his prime.

The match required some bureaucratic juggling. Whites wanting to watch needed to apply for permits, and security around the Lions was tight, although the police presence in the township was discreet. The scribes were taken directly from their beachfront hotel to the Sisa Dukashe Stadium in kombis. All except for Reason of the *Daily Telegraph*. 'I went up to the ground in a specially hired corporation bus,' he wrote, preferring to spend the time leading up to the match with friends and a group of travelling Welsh fans rather than the funky tabloid lowlife.

Once at the ground, the press sorted out their communications issues with the local Post Office officials, who had telex machines on hand in the bowels of what by now was a stadium simmering with excitement. Despite the unpopularity of the contest in more radical political quarters, it was still a Tuesday to remember in a township not used to receiving northern-hemisphere guests. The full crowd was entertained with an early curtain-raiser between an Eastern Cape Railways XV and the Border Colts, and at 2 p.m. with a match between Gompo Union and Zwelitsha Union. After that came the drum majorettes dressed in white dresses with purple capes, white boots and white berets. They made a sparklingly proud guard of honour for the Lions, who were led out by McBride, holding the trademark furry lion above his head. With the third Test only four days away, playing was a gesture of respect by the captain, although the team he headed was undoubtedly of the mix-and-match variety. Bennett and Edwards, the Test pair, were the halfbacks, but the front row (with Carmichael, Kennedy and Burton) was second choice, and the rest of the pack had an improvised look about it, with David, Ralston and Ripley all starting. Before the festivities were completely over, the mayor of the township, Mr A.B. Toyana, attempted to bring the same jazzy charm to proceedings that had been provided by the drum majorettes. 'May I, in the same breath, as first citizen of Mdantsane, praise the British Lions as a team as well as individuals for their gallant and audacious stand to come forth and make a contribution towards a nation-building project,' he said. 'It is on that score that I boldly say that blacks and whites present today will bear testimony to the compilers of the golden book of the black nation in South Africa.'

In pure rugby terms, the entry in the golden book is a short one. The Leopards were beaten 56-10, conceding 10 tries, the Lions doing what they had done so often before in scoring heavily in the second half – 39 points in this case. So mangled were the Leopards in the tight phases that they frequently pleaded with referee Steve Strydom to take pity on them and award the Lions something other than a scrum. As the match progressed, it had an increasingly lopsided feel. Many years afterwards, Cushe was still moved to wail: 'We wanted to play just like Fiji, but we couldn't because we were beaten in the scrums. It was the toughest game of my life.'

Despite playing in a beaten pack, Cushe was on the prowl. He pounced on a long throw that sailed over the back of the Lions lineout and ran downfield, passing to Tsotsobe, one of the successes of the Italian tour. The winger was felled close to the line, and, unfortunately, the Leopards were unable to score. Cushe continued to scavenge and, later in the match, snatched the intercept he had long been eyeing. 'I noticed that they had only five forwards in the maul and the loose trio would hang back,' he said. 'It was going okay, and then I realised that Edwards, who had a good long pass, would go directly to the loose forwards, missing out Bennett. They were on our 22 and I went for an intercept because I was now marking them and I was successful. I went. I was tackled by Andy Irvine. I passed to Charles [Mgweba], who scored our one try.'

With local try-scoring in short supply against the Lions, Mgweba's try was celebrated as an act of heroism and audacity. There had been some debate in the Leopards camp beforehand about their system of play, with Amos du Plooy, their advisor, arguing for a more conservative pattern, while the Leopards wanted to spin the ball from hand to hand and gallop downfield like the rugby magicians they believed themselves to be. The Mgweba try was something of a vindication, not only for the players against the old Springbok, but for expression and style of play. Those 30 000 present were keenly aware that up until then the Springboks had not scored against the Lions, and that provincial tries against them, with none by the Orange Free State or Northern Transvaal, were becoming rarer than a smile from Prime Minister Vorster. The symbolism of the score rose glistening from the game as something to treasure. 'When we scored that try it was as though we had won,' said Cushe. 'It was just so beautiful.'

The fans were not the only ones to celebrate Cushe. In the press facilities at the back of the grandstand, Reason found himself inspired. In a syndicated *Telegraph* piece for the *Sunday Times* the following Sunday, he was full of praise. 'When Cushe first cut through the middle of the field against the Lions in Mdantsane, the whole concept of non-white rugby in South Africa shot forward, as in fact he did,' he wrote. 'The Welsh called Dai Morris "The Shadow", even though he is as white as a sheet, but this black shadow called Cushe stuck so close to the Lions with the ball for so long he looked as if he was permanently attached to them.' Reason was a man with a nimble mind, so this might simply have been a veiled way of saying Cushe spent much of the match either in an offside position or close to it. Then again, maybe not, for he continued in less ambiguous fashion: 'I have not seen seven flankers better than Morgan Cushe on this tour. If he can play as well as he did against the Lions, despite his lack of top-class competition, he could go a very long way indeed. Who knows, Cushe may turn out to be even more important in the history of South African sport than Basil D'Oliveira.'

As a rugby player, Cushe was not as disadvantaged as some, but his disadvantage was still profound. His friend Swartz, who travelled to Italy, played against the Lions and eventually joined him at Swallows after spells with local clubs College and Excelsior, told of what torture it was for them to play on un-grassed fields 'like corrugated roads'. The uprights and crossbars in their matches were frequently wooden, and sometimes the players laced together old samp sacks to provide a rudimentary fence around the ground for spectators. 'Friends used to snatch up dirt for my kicking tee,' remembered Swartz. 'They used to plead with me to get it over. Scoring a try was always so painful because you had to dive [on gravel].'

For players like Swartz and Cushe, rugby was largely invisible toil. There were certainly opportunities (according to the SA Rugby annual's historian, Paul Dobson, Cushe played 19 'Tests' from 1972 to 1980), yet these took place in segregated South Africa, where freedom of movement and association was severely restricted. Were Cushe to have had a beer or two with a white man after one of his Tests, there would have been precious few places in which to do so; were he to travel home by bus to his poor man's house in the township, he would have had to take the Putco from a segregated taxi rank and not the Greyhound.

In 1975, Cushe played for a President's XV against France at Newlands; in 1979 he was part of a highly successful SA Barbarians side under Chick Henderson and Dougie Dyers to England; and a year later he captained the Leopards in a mid-week fixture against Billy Beaumont's Lions, although in that particular game the dirt-trackers were captained by Welshman Derek Quinnell. The fact that he could play for a black invitation side against the Lions in fixtures six years apart attests to the degree to which sport in South Africa at the time had fossilised, pressed flat in its racially defined underworld. Cushe's opportunities were no more than crumbs tossed from the white man's table, shop-window fixtures intended to depict progress while inadvertently showing that South African sport was horribly stuck.

The deeper tragedy of Cushe's career was that he had neither the wherewithal nor the expanded cultural horizons of a D'Oliveira. Cutting a path to England from Uitenhage would have been completely alien, because there were no pioneers before him. Cushe's world was the small provincial universe of the semi-rural Eastern Cape, a cruel universe, but a familiar and emotionally replenishing one all the same. There were also no benefactors or fixers (as there were in D'Oliveira's case with, say, John Arlott) to smooth the journey. Reason's hope for Cushe was well meaning, but circumstances were such that the flank, who ironically styled himself on Jan Ellis by also carrying the ball in one hand, would never be as successful or as well known as D'Oliveira. There was also a sticky human truth involved in Cushe not considering a life elsewhere. He was full of showmanship, graced with the perversity of the maverick: many in the community of Kwanobuhle adored him, and he stood to lose much by leaving. Apartheid South Africa was incapable of providing him with a fair present, let alone a fair future, as either a human being or a rugby player. The best that it could offer were Tuesday afternoons with drum majorettés, trips to Italy and the admiration of highbrow journalists. He was a man compromised by the sinister co-option politics of the times. There are even small examples – such as his tart dismissal of Craven as 'somebody who knew me' – to suggest that he was painfully aware of just that.

It was all very well for Reason to talk blithely of Cushe as rugby's possible D'Oliveira, but the Lions touring party, picked from multicultural seventies Britain, was itself an all-white one. There were substantial immigrant communities in urban Britain in the mid-seventies, particularly in English cities like London, Birmingham and Leeds, and although they would have gravitated more naturally towards cricket with their Caribbean and Asian roots, there is little to suggest any interest in them from the rugby establishment or the public schools, the cradles of the game in England and Scotland. We only have to look at the reaction from within the West Indian section of the crowd at the Oval after witnessing Viv Richards' 291 in the fifth Test against England in 1976 to realise that racial harmony was not all that it should have been in London that summer. There were race riots at the Notting Hill Carnival (commemorated by The Clash in their song 'White Riot') and, a year later, in Lewisham, a mixed borough south of the Thames, the right-wing National Front decided to stage a highly provocative march with nasty results. Against the backdrop of these kinds of racial tensions playing themselves out in the United Kingdom, there is something thoughtlessly convenient in the British press corps' occupation of their cheery perch on the high moral ground. Although well meaning, there is a paternalism in Reason's implicit invitation to Cushe to jump ship, a kind of 'come across to us, they can't take care of you here' attitude, when the emergence of a black Lion like Jeremy Guscott or, say, England's Victor Ubogu or Courtney Lawes, was so obviously far into the future. The terrible reality of it all was that the Lions went home, leaving Cushe behind. They came back six years later, again played the Leopards, and again left him behind. Contrary to what Mayor Toyana had hoped for in his pre-match address, it was not exactly a glorious passage in 'the golden book of the black nation'.

After retiring, Cushe was employed by the Eastern Province Rugby Union as a development officer for 17 years, doing what he could to keep the game as vibrant as it had been in his day, when teams like Boiling Water and Winter Rose flourished in the Eastern Cape. After being in and out of hospital for months, he finally succumbed to renal failure in late 2013, dying aged 65. I took slight comfort from the fact that when I interviewed him at the Wild Rapids Spur in Uitenhage before he died, after having driven through the windswept miseries of Fugard country one Saturday morning to get there, he ordered the 'Trailblazer Breakfast'. He was a man who must have lived at least some of his interior life in a twilight zone of the heart: alienating some in his community and living with their wrath, yet never being able to do quite enough to become the Springbok he rightly believed he should have been.

Down the road and up a hill, his mate Swartz lives a quietly neglected life in Swallow Drive, an appropriate address for a player who gave so much to the club of the same name. His competitive fire has been dampened, but the glow of the odd ember remains. When I asked him in Cushe's presence who had the better hands, Swartz replied: 'Obviously my hands were better [than Morgan's] and my boot was excellent. I could kick with both my right and my left foot.' When he spoke to us in his cold, tiny lounge, I noticed a large black-and-white photograph of him as a boy hanging high on the wall nearby. Proud and scrubbed clean, buttoned up in his high-school colours blazer, it was a reminder that the world was once fresh with something called promise. Listening to Swartz complain through the morning, sometimes amiably, sometimes a little sourly, was to be reminded that promise was no longer quite so close to hand.

8

Panic in the garden (of Springbok rugby)

HAVING NO IDEA of their best side, the brains trust was now spinning merrily on the treadmill of reactive selecting. Several hours after the Lions' defeat of Northern Transvaal, the five selectors (Johan Claassen, Nelie Smith, Butch Lochner, Daan Swiegers and Ian Kirkpatrick) announced the team to play in the third Test, at Boet Erasmus. It contained 10 changes and a positional switch from the side beaten at Loftus in the second.

Not surprisingly, given that they were caught in a hall of mirrors, the new side was full of Quaggas, Northern Transvalers and Free Staters, those who had most recently given indication that the Lions could be tamed. From the Quaggas, South-Eastern Transvaal's Polla Fourie made his Test debut, as did Johan Kritzinger, who had also had a decent game for Oberholzer's Transvaal against the tourists. John Williams and Kevin de Klerk, the second Test locks, were jettisoned in favour of Orange Free State's Johan de Bruyn and Northern Transvaal's Moaner van Heerden respectively. There were still more changes further forward in that Marais remained but Frederickson did not, being replaced by Piston van Wyk, the Northern Transvaler who had been given such a going-over by Windsor at

Newlands. Despite Windsor's likely glee, there is evidence to support the idea that playing Van Wyk was the correct decision. Not only was he highly regarded by Marais, he also ended up playing in the fourth Test, at Ellis Park, suggesting that after the Frederickson experiment at Loftus, the ground on which Van Wyk would have been at his most comfortable, the selectors had finally stumbled on the best man to do the hooking job. Niek Bezuidenhout, Van Wyk's front-row teammate from Northern Transvaal, kept his place, with Free State's André Bestbier and Rampie Stander providing forward cover as reserves. The press were ambivalent about the changes and perturbed by their number, although they welcomed the addition of players with fire in their belly, like the lock pair of Van Heerden and De Bruyn. They were also quick to seize on the fact that in choosing two 'enforcers' (the term had yet to be coined), the selectors had dispensed with the more athletic lineout talents of, say, a John Williams. The Boks would struggle with lineout ball, predicted the scribes – and they did.

The breezy swing of the axe was equally evident in the backs. Both halfbacks were chopped, the Transvaal pair of Bosch and Bayvel losing their places to Roy McCallum (this was to get complicated in the days leading up to the game) and Jackie Snyman, who played in the centre at Loftus but shuttled across to flyhalf for the Test at Boet Erasmus. Peter Whipp, Snyman's centre partner at Loftus, lost his place and the centre vacancies were filled by Jan Schlebusch, who'd had an eye-catching game for Orange Free State against the visitors, and Peter Cronje, the Transvaal centre who had spent much of the tour battling with a serious shoulder injury. 'I must have had three or four ops on it in the end,' he told me after a middling round at the

Langebaan Golf Club in the early summer of 2013. 'The original injury happened in '73; I re-injured it in '74 and had another operation in '75. First there was a staple, then a bone graft. After that they put a pin in. I played the Test with a special orthopaedic strap underneath the jersey. I couldn't move my right arm much above the horizontal.'

Tonie Roux, who had not caught a game for Northern Transvaal against the Lions because the Northerns selectors had plumped for Chris Luther's kicking ability instead, replaced Ian McCallum at fullback. The wings for Boet Erasmus were Chris Pope, an ever-present throughout the series, and Transvaal's Gert Muller, a man who, like Van Wyk, was making a comeback after playing the first Test at Newlands. From the scribes there was a kind of grudging acceptance of those selected leavened by something resembling blind hope. They carefully pointed out that, without Gerald Bosch, the Springboks (or '*ons Bokkies*' as *Rapport*'s Zaayman was fond of calling them) were unlikely to kick anything out of Snyman's 40-metre range and the combinations were untested. Bosch and Bayvel at least had the advantage of playing together for both Diggers and Transvaal. The same could not be said of Snyman and Roy McCallum, although, as fate would have it, McCallum did not end up as Snyman's scrumhalf at all. Claassen rounded off the shambles by saying directly after the team was announced that 'here was a team to take to the Border'. He was not wrong; Springbok rugby was indeed on a war footing. The problem was how the Boks were going to fight the war. Brute strength was not the answer, and they did not have the cohesion or the confidence in the backs to breech the Lions' line. It all looked rather like the men of Springbok rugby were queuing up to witness another disaster.

The Lions' selection dilemmas were not of quite the same

scale, although there were issues around Bennett, Irvine, Ralston and Brown. Bennett's only game since the second Test had been against the Leopards. Cushe had noticed Edwards passing the ball directly to his loose forwards in that game without realising that it was more pragmatic than tactical, because Bennett's gashed foot hurt. Photographs taken at the beginning of the match show strapping on both his knees. He ran gingerly at Boet Erasmus once the Lions arrived in Port Elizabeth, and the concerns lingered. Would Gibson play at 10? Might McGeechan? Or would the nursing and care mean that the sparkling Bennett was all right on the night? It transpired that he was, and the Bennett–Edwards combination was reunited for the first time since the second Test, in Pretoria.

The Brown situation was slightly more complicated. It was assumed that Ralston would replace Brown if the knee injury the Scottish lock had sustained against Northern Transvaal did not clear up in time, but it all became a little irrelevant when Ralston was punched with such ferocity in the Leopards game that some of his teeth pierced his cheek. He was already suffering dental problems, having had teeth loosened in the Quaggas game, and through the latter part of the week it was touch-and-go as to whether either one would play. Brown was having none of it. He realised that the match was going to be the most significant of his career and he was not prepared to miss out. He was joined in the side by his Scottish teammate Irvine, who had impressed with his long-range kicking and spirited counter-attacking. Many felt that with the possible exception of Cushe, Irvine was the best player on the field in Mdantsane, and he replaced his colleague Billy Steele in a backline that was as settled as the salt in the pans outside the city.

The night before the game was when McBride uttered his

famous 'You ain't seen nothing yet' quote, partly as a boast, but also as a cheerful and convivial stating of the obvious. *Volksblad*'s Van Zyl, who was in the bar of the Marine Hotel with McBride and a handful of journalists at the time, recalled it all clearly. 'It was almost like yesterday, I can still see him there telling the press men, definitely,' he said. 'It was a modest form of bragging. We can improve and we still have a couple of things up our sleeve is what he was saying.'

With McBride entertaining the journalists in the bar, Trevor Quirk could not help but take a reading on his emotional barometer: the Lions were relaxed, passing out their ticket allocations and chatting to people from home. Some were in the bar and some outside, taking in the sea air after their visit to the aquarium earlier that afternoon to see and feed the famous smiling dolphins, Dimple and Haig. 'There was such an aura of confidence about them,' he said. 'There they were, milling around their hotel, having a couple of beers in the bar. The Springbok management would have put them to bed and Dawie de Villiers would have said a prayer in a similar situation with the Boks.'

The Springboks' preparation, meanwhile, had been less than ideal. As the week progressed it became clear that Roy McCallum was not going to pass muster because of an injury (some say knuckle, some finger) and that either Boland's Barry Wolmarans, Griquas' Gert Schutte or Orange Free State's Gerrie Sonnekus would have to do the scrumhalf job instead. Cronje remembers a bizarre situation one afternoon late in the week, when the three possible scrumhalves and the backline players were ordered to the ballroom of Port Elizabeth's Marine Hotel. Tables and chairs were cleared and the players were ordered to take off their shoes and form up in a line, 'walking through' a move as they would have in the Test. Schutte, Wolmarans and Sonnekus were all given opportunities to see what they could do, with Jackie Snyman standing alongside at flyhalf. In slow motion, each of them passed the ball down the line and returned to do exactly the same thing in the opposite direction once they had reached the ballroom's end.

'"Right," Claassen and the selectors told us, "we've seen enough, we'll announce the side in half an hour's time,"' remembers Cronje, as the selectors plumped for the inexperienced Sonnekus, partly because he'd had a decent game for Orange Free State two weeks before. Bayvel says that his pulled hamstring put him out of the reckoning, although he reserves a barb. 'It got out that I couldn't pass left to right standing and Gerrie Sonnekus could, so he got in,' he told me. 'The Lions were just screaming with laughter.'

The Test itself was neither as humbling nor as eye-catchingly disastrous as the Loftus game had been for the home side. Unlike the five tries they had conceded at Loftus, the Springboks only leaked three at Boet Erasmus, one of them an almost laughably simple dive-over after a lineout close to the Bok line; another a passage of late opportunism by J.J. Williams to truly seal the Springboks' fate. The score when Williams dashed over for the Lions' third try was 19-6 to the Lions, and although the Springboks were not going to win it, they had at least kept the score within manageable proportions.

Damage limitation was not uppermost in the Springboks' minds when they had sprinted down the tunnel approximately an hour and a half earlier, the Lions waiting patiently for them on the field, doing their warm-up exercises and trying to remain calm. Legend has it that the Boks were late because Koornhof had delivered the pre-match team talk, thoughtfully giving men like the mean De Bruyn the benefit of the government's point of view. Claassen and Marais denied this, the former Springbok captain rejecting it vehemently. He made the point that Craven was a *bloed-Sap*, an old Jan Smuts, Sir De Villiers Graaff and United Party man, and as such would never have allowed the minister of sport anywhere near the change rooms. Le Roux agreed with Marais' *bloed-Sap* analysis, adding that as a result of his authority and the esteem in which he was held, Craven had managed to negotiate space between himself and both the National Party and the Broederbond, cleverly keeping them at arm's length through a combination of flattery and persuasion. 'He [Craven] hated the whole Broederbond thing,' said Le Roux. 'But they kept him there because he had the enthusiasm and the rugby knowledge. No one else could do the job.'

Looking back on the Test it seems almost tidal, the one side sweeping downfield only to be repulsed; the current of the match suddenly moving in the opposite direction. For all the brutal ebb and flow, there is something frustratingly inconclusive about much of the match. The Boks are almost wild on adrenaline; crazy men ready to run through buildings rather than just walls. De Bruyn snatches the ball after a kickoff and thumps it downfield, plunging off in pursuit; Kritzinger rushes for the Lions line and is pulled down close, collapsing under a red avalanche, his team appealing for the try as a flurry of punches are thrown. Jackie Snyman weasels his way into space, gaining a few precious yards before being yanked down. All this suggests courage, wilfulness, pluck; what it does not suggest is rugby intimacy, the telepathic sense of knowing someone is running a line inside of you without you having to look, or having the instinct to throw deep into the lineout in a certain situation because such a throw has worked well for you before.

At the end of it all there is something gauche about the Springboks' performance, something haphazard and unconvincing. Snyman seems unable to successfully kick the ball 10 metres after kickoff and the Lions' first try, to the effervescent Brown, is almost vaudevillian, with Marais throwing in, Brown poaching and rolling over from close, the bemused Springboks looking on mildly aghast, as though they have been victims of a con man who has tricked them in the same way before. Only the Lions' second try has the magic of stardust, a regulation first-phase lineout take with the ball skipping down the line. It eventually finds its way to J.J. Williams, who has found the space to ghost past his defender around the outside; he covers ground and with options running out, he flips it cleverly inside to J.P.R. Williams, who keeps the move alive long enough for J.J. to loop around him and receive another inside pass. He snakes through on the angle and scores underneath the posts.

As ever on the tour, the Lions pack never takes a backward step. They are immovable on their own throw and slyly destructive on that of the Boks, wheeling, disrupting and counter-shoving to great effect. All these years later, Cronje has the idea that at some point during the match he felt that the Boks could actually win the Test, and, in a strange way, this does not seem quite as far-fetched as it might at first appear. The individual Boks are certainly courageous, and there is a period in the approach to halftime where the match seems to be wobbling on its axis, unsure of which way to fall. Yet there is no cohesion, no team ethic from the Boks, and so Cronje's statement only makes sense in a limited way, because at Boet Erasmus the Springboks were 15 primed individuals in search of an ethic, while the Lions were a team obsessively in search of a series victory.

Many years later, Fourie, the debut flank, talked about the Boks' heroic mindlessness. 'We were like lost sheep,' he told Christo Lemmer, making the point that the boys played for the team and the country but not for one another. It being his debut Test, his experience was not unlike that of Germishuys, who had played in his debut at Loftus, the first 25 minutes passing in a whirl, the action telescoped into tight passages of action, difficult to make sense of in any kind of broad perspective. Fourie was so on edge that he had not slept the night before, and so played the game in a fugue of nervous exhaustion. 'It was not that we lacked for motivation – a Springbok team never lacks for motivation – it was just that we were like a bunch of outsiders who didn't even know each other,' he said.

The Lions were angling for their fourth try (and might almost have scored it) when referee Cas de Bruyn blew the final whistle. With the series pocketed, McBride was carried off the field shoulder-high. He paused to wave and thank the rest of his Lions, who were sitting opposite him in the grandstand. Marais showed touching dignity in lingering. While most of the Springboks trooped off, only too happy to put distance between themselves and disaster, he waited to shake hands and say a few words of congratulations. Although a straightforward act, in the mayhem it proved surprisingly difficult to do.

Like the Western Province versus Lions game, the third Test is best encapsulated in a photograph rather than words. If everything that needed to be said was condensed into the image of Ripley bearing down on Roy McCallum at Newlands, so the summary of the third Test was to be found in the image of J.J. Williams sprinting past a despairing defender for the Lions' third try. On closer inspection we can see that it was Marais who lunged a fraction of a second too late. Reluctantly recalled and pushed into service aged 33, the man who lifted stones in an effort to get fit (the persistent Old Testament echoes) is too ponderous for the quicksilver Williams. Shoddy timing is not confined to Marais, the man who hopped on the milk train rather than the express. The selectors have stumbled upon their best combinations – and so their best side – far too late in the series; the Springbok fans have woken up to the technical brilliance of the Lions' front five when they have already wreaked their havoc; the referees have woken up to the Lions' quick-wittedness and gamesmanship far too late; the public at large have taken an inordinate amount of time in coming to terms with the Lions' streak of ruthlessness; the list could go on.

Despite Marais' tenacity, there is a deeper hopelessness embodied in the photograph – the absence of the rugby ball. As we know, the ball has bounced unkindly for the Boks all series. The photograph captures unluckiness or, better put, lucklessness, because in this case the bounce of the ball has been so wicked that *it is not there any more.* This pushes Marais' grasping lunge into a completely different section of the arrival's hall. If degrees of lateness could be quantified, Marais, missing both man and ball, is as late as it is humanly possible to be. In a way, the subject of the photograph transmutes before our very eyes. Instead of an image of speed, it is an image of Williams's *speed of thought.* And how easily the individual example can stand for the whole; how, like a synecdoche, the Williams try

can stand in for a series in which the Springboks were not only outpaced on the field, but outfoxed within the confines of that far larger and more frightening expanse, the mind.

There is more to say about the photograph. In the upper edge of the frame, behind a wooden fence supporting a roll of barbed wire, sits a group of coloured supporters. In front of them, on the field itself, is a group of four or five black policemen. All of them, the coloureds and the policemen, are cheering Williams. One policeman is doing a quick jig, a dance of delight. But the crowd and the cops are not only cheering for Williams. They are cheering *against* Marais. Never have the traumas of apartheid sport been so graphically and memorably illustrated. Reduced to its essence, this is what playing sport in the apartheid state meant: having a portion of the crowd who should be supporting you supporting the opposition and cheering when you lose.

In so many ways, the photograph is a full stop. It essentially shows the end of the series, because although there was a Test yet to play, the series had been won by the Lions. In retrospect, it also signals an end to the wilfully blind experimentation embarked upon by the selectors, as the Springboks turned a corner in drawing the final Test 13-all. What remained open and unfinished were the terrible divisions in South African society, wounds that to this day have still not healed. The match on the paddock might have been definitive, but there was no such closure for society as a whole. Men like Cushe would not be allowed to play for the Springboks, certainly not as the 1970s progressed; and the Springboks themselves would only be supported by a segment of the population. Other race groups and constituencies would support them under sufferance, while the more radical would either boycott their matches or actively support their opposition.

According to a demure and almost apologetic little article in *The Star* on the following Monday, the Lions drank 65 bottles of champagne through Saturday night and Sunday morning. The article failed to mention what else they consumed, or the fact that the Lions became so drunk and disorderly that they started ripping curtains off their rails and tossing them into a fire made on a table in the team room. The manager of the Marine Hotel finally called the police, and this resulted in the famous Lions' set-piece where McBride, having been roused by Brown, wanders out into the corridor in his underpants, takes a ruminative pull on his pipe, and asks the manager how many policemen he thinks there will be. *The Star*'s anonymous correspondent put the damage at R450, a substantial sum in those days, but one probably significantly wide of the mark. 'We were not unduly concerned,' Mr Baumker, one of the hotel owners, was quoted as saying. 'After they had won the series we expected some damage ... We would welcome them back.'

Perhaps the long-suffering Baumker had a point. The Lions certainly did not corner the market on riotous behaviour. Andy Leslie's All Blacks would march through East London two years later, flattening the crops and carrying off the women. Such behaviour was almost expected, a given of touring. Bad behaviour was commonplace in the rock 'n' roll world of the period. Keith Moon, The Who's drummer, once quipped: 'I don't give a damn about Holiday Inn rooms because there are ten million of them the world over, all exactly the same.'

The Lions never forgot Marais' dignity, and he was invited to all the anniversary dinners in the United Kingdom. Although the hurt remains, the shame has softened. 'Every time I suffered difficulty I tried to make the best use of negative things,' Marais told me. 'That '74 defeat took me 21 years to make sense of. Choet and his wife and my wife and I had two dinners in the years afterwards, and on the 20th anniversary [of the Lions tour] Hansie [Cronje]'s side played at the Oval at the same time and we were invited to the Long Room. John Major was there and we met him and Hansie and it was very pleasant and we had a nice chat. We also had dinners in all four capitals. In Edinburgh I sat next to Princess Anne. She knew more about rugby than you and I did. Out of defeat can come something very useful.'

On one trip north, Marais took the skins of four springboks with him, an echo of what had happened in 1974, when the Lions were frequently asked to sign springbok skins. 'Those springboks were shot in the head, which was significant because, symbolically, that's exactly what happened to us.' He also flogged his Springbok blazer, receiving R70 000 for it from a British collector. It was clearly not a tour that inspired the hoarding of mementoes.

After the madness in the Marine Hotel, the Lions could barely muster the enthusiasm to climb aboard an aircraft, let alone pull on the red jersey. As a consequence, their first match after the third Test, against Border in East London, was possibly their worst performance of the tour, with the exception of their early match against South West Africa. Their collective *babbelas* was not helped by the wind howling through the Basil Kenyon Stadium, although such was the cachet of the fixture that a desperate section of the crowd perched on the limbs of the coral trees outside, much like they would at a Caribbean cricket ground. The match itself was a slow-burning affair, with Bennett, still suffering from the after-effects of the injury he had sustained in the second Test, crying off shortly beforehand to be replaced by the ever-willing McGeechan. Watched by the Natal captain, Tommy Bedford, and Basil Kenyon himself, the Lions edged unconvincingly in front (10-3 at halftime) before loping away with it in the second half to win 26-6. Tries came from Edwards and Steele (two), with Irvine helping himself to four penalties and a conversion. Border's flyhalf, Joel Steenkamp, scored his side's six points from two penalties.

For Border, the partisan crowd was kept ever hopeful by a good game from their scrumhalf, Chicken Gendall, and their trio of loosies, George Willson, Derek Neale-May and Keith Watt, although Kirkpatrick, the national selector, commented afterwards that he had seen nothing to indicate that Border was a hidden Springbok gold mine. Despite being finally outgunned, and having nothing in their armoury the equivalent of the inspirational Edwards, Border did not lack for pluck. 'Not only did Border show courage,' wrote Shafto in *The Star* on the following day, 'they also showed considerable cheek in packing only a front row on a number of occasions against the Lions' steamroller pack. What is more, the tactic worked, for it had the effect of forcing the Lions to hold back their shove to stabilise the scrum.'

With the match stretching the Lions' unbeaten streak to 19 matches, the thrills happened not in the stadium but on the way there. The tourists' flight out of Port Elizabeth had to be aborted because a bird or birds flew into the 737's engine and, just to be sure, the pilot turned the aircraft around. Windsor and some pals were not about to tempt fate again, and so decided to hire a kombi and drive to East London instead. Combustion, though, was not confined to the aircraft's wings. In the aeroplane itself, weeks of animosity finally flared up between journalists John Reason and Terry O'Connor. They worked for different newspapers, had very different styles and worldviews, and disagreed about virtually everything they cared to discuss. Matters between them suddenly burst into flames somewhere just outside of Port Elizabeth, because Shafto remembers looking up from his seat in the aircraft and seeing the two journalists squaring up in the aisle. The confrontation certainly seemed in character for the naturally combative O'Connor, but less so for Reason, who, unlike Terry and his knuckleduster prose, was no stylistic slugger but rather a man of careful blows and deft jabs. Shafto does not remember if the men were separated or even who landed the first punch, but he does remember the astounded silence that greeted the spectacle. 'Everyone's eyes were fixed on them,' Shafto said. 'Reason was always a bit of a don. I don't know if he was an Oxford or a Cambridge man, but Reasie didn't like O'Connor. It was a class thing. They fought all the time. They always had opposite views on everything.'

It was generally a time of bad tempers and frayed nerves. Hollings Norton, the Natal lock, told me that he had never been punched as much as he was during their game against the Lions the week after the third Test, the visitors' 20th game and the third last of the tour. Norton generously took this to be a case of mistaken identity because he was blond, as was Tommy Bedford, his skipper, and Norton suspected that some of the punishment meted out to him was really directed at Bedford. Not that Bedford, the controversial eighthman and, according to a Natal journalist who covered the game, 'a shit-stirrer of note', escaped injury. The Lions were 9-6 ahead with only 10 minutes to play when it was decided that the most profitable route to a more convincing victory would be to deal with the talismanic Bedford once and for all. He was singled out for brutal treatment first by J.P.R. Williams, whom he had tackled into touch. Williams responded by pummelling Bedford as he lay on the ground curled up in the foetal position, and had to be pulled off by a spectator. The 'referee' in this instance was Alex Bridger, a detective sergeant in the Railways Police. He himself was a rugby player, and had been suspended for 18 months in 1972 'following an incident with a referee'. Having lived through similar situations on the rugby field, Bridger was not about to stand by and watch Williams at work. 'I have been involved in incidents on the rugby field myself and I can understand the fullback's reaction if he had been hurt,' Bridger said at the time. 'But it incensed me to see him strike a defenceless man. Tommy was on the ground, completely defenceless. If I didn't restrain Williams, he may have carried on for too long.'

The Lions did not leave it at that. At the next lineout, Bedford's arms were pinned behind his back and Fran Cotton thrashed him. The referee, Piet Robbertse, who played an inordinate amount of injury time in the second half, punished neither incident. In the 11 minutes of injury time, the Lions stockpiled an amazing 21 points against the weary young men from Natal, finally winning the match 34-6. Bedford said afterwards that Robbertse had played such a grotesquely long period of injury time because he had wanted to weasel his way into the Lions' hearts – as it was they who would pick the home referee for the final Test after being presented with a list by the SA board. It was a plausible theory, although one contradicted by events. Max Baise refereed the fourth Test, at Ellis Park, his performance notable for its flakiness. If the Natal match was anything to go by, it is unlikely that Robbertse would have performed any better.

The conformist world of South African rugby in the sixties and seventies was not an environment in which Bedford was naturally comfortable. Almost out of reflex he clashed with the lords of the game (he called them the 'grass chair brigade') as he waged a running battle against all facets of small-mindedness. Although sometimes stroppy, he was remarkably consistent in his views, particularly his political ones, and was a brave, lightweight flank who had no alternative but to try to outwit his opponents because he was unable to flatten them. After making his debut as a 19-year-old for Natal in 1961, he found himself playing for the Boks against the Wallabies two years later, and went on to form a highly successful back row with Piet

Greyling and Frik du Preez. 'He was remarkably quick – I saw him run around a provincial wing in a game in Pietermaritzburg – and he had an instinctive feel for the game,' recalled the *Natal Witness*'s John Bishop. 'He played for an incredible 15 years. He lost much of his pace, but he has always been a deep thinker about the game. Natal during his time always fielded small forwards and played with little possession. Tom, and Izak van Heerden and Keith Oxlee [the Natal coaches], offset this by using tricks, changes of direction, and speeding up the game as they tried to battle brawn with brains. So often they succeeded. In 1963, I think, they went through the season unbeaten, but there was no Currie Cup at stake because of the Wallaby tour.'

Bedford may have been physically assaulted by the Lions in the match, but in the weeks preceding the fixture he had been bruised more deeply by the selectors' lack of interest in both himself and young Natal players like hooker John Trollope, Mark McKenzie and fullback Malcolm Swanby. Trollope was technically excellent and coped with the brutalities of the Lions scrum by hooking the ball with his head, as he was pushed so low. When the packs broke up and he and Bobby Windsor, his opposite number, were trotting after the ball, Windsor mentioned casually that if Trollope was stupid enough to hook the ball that way again, he would trample all over his face. Trollope thought nothing of it until Windsor acted on his promise at the very next scrum.

Bedford, meanwhile, was not about to allow the gentilities of the post-match cocktail party to get in the way of his anti-establishment rage. Taking to the podium in his black Natal blazer he cleared his throat and pointedly told the selectors: 'I congratulate you on finally finding your way to Durban, welcome, welcome,' whereupon he gave them a two-fingered salute and held the pose for a few provocative seconds too long in case anyone had missed his intent.

He was not finished. He had ripped a *Daily Dispatch* poster off a pole after the Border game in East London and now unfurled it before his audience. 'LIONS AND GIRLS IN NUDE SCRUM' it read, and Bedford explained that finally, in the twilight of the tour, the secret of the Lions' superior scrummaging had been revealed. The Boks and the provinces were simply practising incorrectly. They clearly needed to do so with members of the opposite sex. While Bedford's light-hearted interlude went some way to softening the tone and allowing everyone to relax, June Bedford, Tommy's wife at the time, took matters into her own hands after her husband's speech. She confronted J.P.R. Williams and tore strips off him for his treatment of her hubby. 'It certainly was a day to remember,' wrote Bishop wryly years later. 'For Williams, Bedford and everyone at that reception.' Indeed it was, because there was precious little mingling after the speeches, and the following morning not one Natal player escorted the Lions from their hotel to Durban airport, defying traditional post-match protocol.

It proved an eventful weekend for Williams. His wife, Scillia, was working at the Addington Hospital in Durban at the time and the two had not seen each other for weeks. Williams was paranoid about being seen with her, so they concocted a plan for her to disguise herself before coming into one of the hotel restaurants. 'Imagine our horror and surprise,' said Williams, 'on entering the restaurant to find Willie John and Syd [Millar] at the table opposite. I don't know who was the more embarrassed. They thought I had taken some other woman out for a meal. It was only then that Scillia took off her wig and revealed her true identity.'

With Scillia pursuing her internship at Addington Hospital, Williams was lured south the following season to play for Northlands in the second division alongside his Lions colleagues J.J. Williams and McLauchlan. The three even turned out alongside Bedford for Natal, playing against Eastern Transvaal. 'J.P.R. scored a try against Eastern Transvaal, and a photograph in Reg Sweet's book on the history of Natal rugby shows Tommy [Bedford] patting him on the back,' recalled the union's official historian, Albert Hennop. 'I wouldn't say they were bosom buddies or anything, but they played in that successful game together.'

9

Last legs

WITH THE SERIES won at Boet Erasmus, the tour entered an itchy, unsatisfactory phase. Behaviour both on and off the field declined markedly. After allegations that the Lions had misbehaved in East London as well as Port Elizabeth, Millar was obliged to issue a clarification – of sorts. 'Mr Millar said his team was "probably the best behaved touring side of all time. The total damage [in East London] was less than R50. It was the first time anything had been broken on tour. If R50 damage is a front page story, then the reporter involved must have been stuck for something to write about,"' wrote Shafto in *The Star* as the boys landed in Durban. 'Mr Millar said a chair and a bed had been damaged but would not detail the events. "The boys were in bed by 11 o'clock that night and, as for girls, I never saw any," he said.'

In fairness, Millar's mealy-mouthed response was a rare instance of evasion from tour management. He and his skipper realised that despite the demob mayhem and the loosening of discipline, they were still obliged to keep the party keen and interested. It was a difficult job: the series could not be taken from them and motivation was slowly ebbing away. Still, it was important to keep some sort of rhythm. They spent much of the time before the Natal match on the beach, enjoying the mild winter sunshine, playing scratch games of football, fishing, and larking around. Photographs taken in the days before the game against Natal show McBride striding through the shallows like a mighty Neptune, smiling broadly and clutching a young ray or sand shark by the tail. This aside, time was dragging in a manner it had not before. Having started in early May, the tour was well over two months old. The men were thinking of other things.

One evening Welsh winger Geoff Evans and English prop Mike Burton were invited by a local chapter of Round Table to have a meal at an Indian beachfront restaurant. The evening was well spent and enjoyable, but the Round Tablers vanished when the bill arrived. The Lions were not going to be saddled with paying and scattered, only to be chased by the establishment's heavies. Burton takes up the story: 'As the first bouncer ran down the corridor after us, Geoffrey stood full-square and caught him with a crushing right, whereupon the other two fell over him. One banged his head on the wall and moaned into semi-consciousness, while the other one accidentally banged his head on Geoff's knee and rendered himself as useless as the fellow lying under him, who had stopped the right hook in the first place.' Having made their escape, tiptoeing over a pile of arms and legs, the two congratulated themselves on their bravery. Breathing more easily as they negotiated their way home. Evans was not watching where he was going and fell into a drain. According to Burton he needed to be extricated from 'an 18-inch sewer' with filth running halfway up his trouser leg.

Despite the fact that many wanted to return to summertime Britain, wives, girlfriends and the comforts of home, there had been structures in place since the beginning of the tour. With Visser playing a key role, the team's senior management had, for example, come up with a sort of council-of-elders-cum-fines-and-disciplinary committee called 'The Mafia'. Featuring McBride, Millar, Slattery and McLauchlan, with Visser occupying the coveted position of 'Godfather', they sat with an air of great mock-dignity about once a week. For meetings they wore black silk shirts, white ties and sunglasses, dispensing justice with a laugh, a pat on the back and another Castle. McBride enjoyed his role immensely (as did McLauchlan) for it gave him licence to be a captain in another guise. He was highly attuned to nuance and mood, and being a member of The Mafia gave him an opportunity to watch his henchmen and lieutenants in ways he could not at practice or on the field.

If anything financial or logistical needed sorting out, The Mafia was called upon to sit and deliberate. As the capo, Visser was never far from his famous briefcase. He controlled the ticket allocations given by the SA board to the Lions and would frequently sell tickets to Lions supporters on their behalf. He kept the money and used it to buy the players trinkets, homecoming gifts and curios. By the end of the tour there were so many calabashes, miniature assegai-and-shield sets and other standard items of the curio trade that the board hired a large box to ship everything from Cape Town to Southampton. Aside from African curios, Visser was also domestically inclined. Stockpiling the ticket-allocation money as he quietly accumulated rands throughout the trip, he managed to buy some of the players and their wives kitchen appliances, even fridges, although how these were returned home will forever remain a mystery.

The tour was also kept alive in its final phase by the extroverts, the dirt-trackers and the anonymous good men who saw the necessity of sacrificing their own needs for those of the team. Windsor, for instance, had started the tour full of social apprehension. He had left school at 15, played football before discovering rugby (his 56 goals in the Newport schools league remained a record for years) and was not cut from the same social cloth as, say, Neary or even Ripley. McBride saw this and he and senior management charmed from the Welsh hooker something like his true self, as chirpy and gregarious off the field as he was nasty and mean upon it. Late into the tour – some claim it was as the team was leaving East London to travel to Port Elizabeth for the third Test – Alun Thomas, the team manager, was presented with a telephone bill for R1 500. Thomas was notoriously absent-minded and was forever leaving keys, items of clothing and wallets, even tickets, wherever the Lions were last. Calls had been made from his room to numbers in Britain, he explained, and he wanted to know who had made them. He confronted the team as they were getting seated on the team bus and became progressively more irate when no one would own up. Eventually he announced that he had asked reception for an itemised bill – and the prefix indicated that the calls had been made to Wales. That, of course, ruled out the majority of the side, although it left the nine Welshmen – including Windsor – as suspects. Still no one was prepared to own up, so Thomas was reluctantly forced to further narrow things down. The calls were made to Pontypool, he announced, and waited for the response. 'Which one of you bastards has been phoning my wife then?' blurted Windsor, unable to contain himself any longer, to hysterical laughter from his teammates.

As the tour progressed, Windsor developed a deserved reputation as a practical joker. So ubiquitous were his gags and so wide was his range of made-up accents that once the team arrived in Johannesburg, he was able to trick Brown without even being directly involved. Brown and Edwards had wanted to play golf with Gary Player since arriving in South Africa, an ambition that was well known within the team. Their schedules somehow failed to dovetail and, what with the Lions getting on and off of planes and Player leaving for (and winning) the British Open, they missed each other for months. Now that Player was back in town after successfully campaigning in Britain, he remembered his promise to the Lions. One weekday morning he put a call through to the Lions' inner-city motel.

'Could I speak to Gordon Brown, please? This is Gary Player.'

'Of course it is, wee Bobby Windsor.'

'Sorry, no, you don't understand, this is GARY PLAYER. I've just returned home after winning the British Open. I would like to play golf against Mr Gordon Brown and Mr Gareth Edwards.'

'I'm sure you would, Bobby. That's a nice South African accent you've got; you're very talented.'

'No, you don't understand, this is the real Gary Player.'

'For the life of me I can't understand why you are playing rugby for Wales when you could be making Mike Yarwood's money. The accent is fantastic. And you know so much about Gary's schedule. I can náe believe you still live in Pontypool.'

'Who do you think this is? I'm telling you, you are speaking to *the* Gary Player.'

Eventually Player managed to convince Brown that he was

not Windsor. Brown alerted his golf-playing mate Edwards, who called in Mike Gibson to make up the missing member in a four-ball. The foursome played at the Killarney Golf Club on the Thursday before the fourth Test. It was meant to be a quiet afternoon affair on a suburban golf course, away from the heaving crowds and prying eyes, but the bush telegraph got working and the golf ended up being watched by hundreds of people, keen to see the Lions and Player in the flesh after his excellent victory over Peter Oosterhuis at Royal Lytham & St Annes the week before. Pairing up with Edwards, Player was in immaculate form, carding a 67. He needed to be because his partner had some early difficulties, according to *Rand Daily Mail*'s Norman Crews: 'Edwards, who obviously prefers the edges of the scrum to hunting the rough of Killarney, set the ball rolling by fluffing his first shot. Whirling round, he pleaded with the gallery, "Can't you shout or sing or do something, I can't play in all this silence."'

The perennially mouthy Edwards was not the only one to encounter unforeseen problems. 'After Gibson had hit a towering iron into the middle of the fairway, he found to his consternation that his ball had been buried in a barrow-load of soft earth,' wrote Crews. '"Gee but you've got big moles in this country," he said.'

Gibson solved his problem and eventually Player and Edwards won four and three. Despite his hand injury, Brown had finally got to play against his hero, thanking him afterwards and telling the reporters present, 'We couldn't have lost to a nicer guy.' Windsor was nowhere in sight.

Player swung both ways – as it were – in the days leading up to the Test. His victory at Royal Lytham was the third of his three British Open victories, and Claassen believed he might be able to inspire a Springbok team who had nothing to lose at Ellis Park. They had finally bottled the selection genie that had eluded them for so long and Player was bound to have something useful to say. His words were indeed inspirational, but, in a sense, might have come from any man off the street. Behind closed doors at the Taylor Travel Lodge in Alberton, he told the Boks that they needed to believe they could win before they could actually do so, adding that the development of South Africa's young rugby players rested on their shoulders. 'I believe you are going to beat the Lions,' he told them. 'You must play on Saturday as though your lives depend on it.'

Player, in his ubiquitous black polo neck and with his caddie 'Rabbit' Dyer, was the most internationally recognisable South African sportsman of the decade, although for an unforgettable season in 1979, Jody Scheckter's Formula One star would shine brightly. He would be victorious in Belgium, Monaco and Italy to win his only drivers' championship, disappearing as quickly as a racing car round a bend. He was some way off from capturing the title in 1974, although this was the year in which he won his first two Grands Prix – in Sweden and Britain – and gained points in eight consecutive races, ranging from the Spanish Grand Prix to the German, in which he finished second in his Tyrrell. At much the same time as Scheckter was working his hot European streak, finishing third in the championship overall, so South African tennis stars Bob Hewitt, Frew McMillan and Bernie Mitton were campaigning in Britain and on the continent, the doubles pair of Hewitt and McMillan winning seven titles in 1974 in venues as far afield as Rotterdam, Montreal and Johannesburg. Their major title of the year was in the World

Doubles in Montreal, where they beat the Australians, Owen Davidson and John Newcombe, in the final. It was not Wimbledon – which they won as a doubles pair in 1967, 1972 and 1978 – but it confirmed their enduring chemistry and uncanny knack for grabbing titles, McMillan and his trademark flat white cap proving to be a perfect foil to Hewitt's temper tantrums.

While the rand had parity with the world's stronger currencies like the pound and the dollar, South Africa was still capable of attracting the odd foreign star. Some had cachet, others less so. Bull Hefer, the wrestling impresario, presented an international wrestling bill at the Portuguese Hall in Turffontein in June at which Spain's José Arroyo took on Apollo, the local man. Tarzan Jacobs tagged on the undercard against Fernando Deschamps of Portugal, and it cost all of 50 cents for the privilege of shouting yourself hoarse from an unreserved seat.

On the other side of town, where the suburbs were quieter, the houses larger and the roads wider, the directors of Jewish Guild football club managed to persuade George Best to make a trip to wintery Johannesburg. Shortly after he arrived, Best was in the stands at the Rand Stadium, watching his new teammates receive a 3-0 drubbing by Rangers, the hard *porras* and Dutchmen from Joburg's south side. The scribes did not need to look far for an explanation. 'Guild suffered from what might accurately be described as an attack of Bestitis,' wrote *Rand Daily Mail*'s Sy Lerman, as he marshalled his alliterations with a heavy hand. 'It was a curious affliction which sapped Guild of their determination, discipline and dedication and reduced them to a meandering and mediocre side. The reason? Best the guest was sitting in the VIP box watching players who were mentally destroyed by his presence.'

One can only wonder what Best would have been able to do against Guild had he signed for Rangers.

After watching the 'meandering and mediocre side' he was about to join, Best ventured into the African sunshine without a hat and got sunstroke. It was so bad that he was forced to miss his first Guild training session, a situation that failed to endear him to either Guild's coach or the members of the club executive who had stumped up the cash to fly him to Johannesburg. There were further intrigues before Best could open his account with Guild: his first training session after recovering from sunstroke was attended by a notorious local stripper. 'A beetroot-burnt George Best had Ultra Violet focussed on him when he resumed training at Balfour Park yesterday afternoon,' wrote Lerman. 'No publicity hound could have dreamed of this gimmick. It had to be coincidence. Yet here was Best, on the day after he was prevented from taking part in his first official practice because of sunburn, face to face with the slinky stripper who has burnt a few fellows in her time.'

Later in the week, Guild and Best rallied. Best's complexion returned to normal and Guild successfully managed to put their nervy performance against Rangers behind them because, on the following Friday, they managed a 1-all draw at home against Hellenic in front of 30 000 supporters. They flew down to Durban on the Saturday and did one better on the Sunday, beating Durban City 2-0, with Best helping Guild striker Bennie Booysen to a brace – to mint a Lerman-like moment of alliterative madness. 'But it was a different story after the changeover [against City] when, like some leprechaun from his native land, he cast a spell over City's vulnerable defence,' wrote an anonymous *Rand Daily Mail* stringer the following day. 'And his magic, even if it only came in short spells, was enough to bring a second goal.'

It was not only the journalists who were inspired. So successful was Best's trip that the original three-match deal was extended. The 1974 FIFA World Cup was about to start in West Germany, football was in the air, and fans had flocked in unprecedented numbers in Cape Town, Durban and Johannesburg to watch the supple, quick-witted Irishman. Through increased gate takings the money was found to pay Best for a fourth game. He stayed out of the sun, and Ultra Violet – real name, Yvonne Wintle – appeared in the Johannesburg Regional Court on a charge of public indecency.

In her way, Wintle was as incorrigible as Best. Once in court it did not take long for her to suggest that the prosecutor might like to see the correct position for her G-string, an offer he politely declined. She denied all the indecency charges, while Best flew home to fritter away a career already on the skids. As Dave Beattie and Terry Lofthouse put it in their *Soccer Scene* column in *The Star* on 13 June: 'Certainly there were some who were among the 30 000 at Rand Stadium, the 22 000 at Green Point stadium, the 10 000 at New Kingsmead (on a wet day) and 8 000 at Balfour Park, who only went to see the man who had gained such a worldwide reputation for his athletic prowess in other directions.'

*

As far as the Springbok team for the fourth Test was concerned, there were changes, but these were in moderation, some being forced on the selectors by circumstance. There were no changes to the backs, with the exception of Sonnekus, who made way for the returning Bayvel. Jackie Snyman was his halfback partner, while the centre pairing of Cronje and Schlebusch remained the same, as did the back trio of Roux at fullback and Pope and Muller on the wings. After Sonnekus's less than brilliant performance at Boet Erasmus, Gareth Edwards was widely quoted in the local press as saying that his pass, too, had once been slow and inaccurate. He had gone away, watched films of Australia's Ken Catchpole and New Zealand's Chris Laidlaw, and had returned a slicker passer of the ball and a far more rounded player. While Edwards was superficially sympathetic, there would in all likelihood have been some private mirth in the Lions camp about the selectors' choice of Sonnekus and the rampant indecision in their ranks – certainly up until the third Test.

While the Bok backline remained largely unchanged, the pack was reshuffled. John Williams's all-round athleticism made up for the more direct and bruising talents of a De Bruyn, and although Van Heerden had gone off clutching his ribs at Boet Erasmus (he was replaced by De Klerk), he was deemed fit enough to play alongside his Northern Transvaal teammate. The front row (Marais, Van Wyk and Bezuidenhout) remained as it had been for the third Test, while Fourie lost his place at openside flanker to Klippies Kritzinger due to a rib injury. Ellis remained, and Kleintjie Grobler slotted into the eighth-man berth vacated by Kritzinger. The side showed a decided Northern bias in containing five Northern Transvalers, four Transvalers and three Free Staters, with Western Province, South West Africa and Eastern Province fielding one player each. It was a remarkable turnaround from the team that had done duty at Newlands, with Coetzee, Whipp and Du Plessis. South

African rugby was clearly returning to a more fundamental template. It was a strong side, a strongly Afrikaans side, and a side that would ultimately do half the business.

The side chosen more or less squared with what Marais claimed in an interview to be his preferred XV. His ideal front row was exactly that of the fourth Test, but, while he agreed on Williams for his ability in the lineout, his choice to partner Williams was De Klerk. Ellis was a constant in both teams, but Marais plumped for Du Plessis and Coetzee as his loose-trio comrades. He was less decisive as far as his selection of backs was concerned, saying that both Ian McCallum and Dawie Snyman had their fans at fullback; for him the Transvaal half-back combination of Bosch and Bayvel was the best choice; and elsewhere he would have found place for Whipp and Cronje in the centre with Muller and Pope on the wings. His was not a side markedly different from the chosen fourth Test side and contained many of the players who, like Marais, would go on to France at the end of the season. In winning there, they would reclaim some of the pride that had been so foolishly thrown away on the Lions' visit.

As for the Lions themselves, Brown was their major concern. He had suffered from knee injuries already on tour, but this time round it was a hand injury with which he was struggling, despite regular daily visits to the physiotherapist. Brown – who once had a Melrose player's tooth surgically removed from his foot – had been a revelation in South Africa. Once Williams had lost his place in the Springbok second row after the second Test, at Loftus Versfeld, he was unsurpassed in the lineouts, taking clean ball from Windsor and making a merry nuisance of himself on the opposition throw and the dark recesses of the tight loose. It was here where his contribution was most significant. Unlike McBride, who, like Marais, was reluctant to throw a punch, Brown was eager to get in touch with the prize-fighter within. While he dished out several blows – he was at his pugnacious best in Port Elizabeth for the provincial game, as well as the third Test – he also suffered for his aggression. At dinner engagements and tour anniversaries afterwards he used to tell the story of being pole-axed by a horrible blow from Van Heerden (or De Bruyn) at Boet Erasmus. The punch was so ferocious that Brown's jaw was knocked out of alignment. He jogged to the next lineout with his head spinning and was pleased to look across at his opposition lock as if to say, 'Was that the best you can do?', a silent question the Springbok apparently found unsettling. Everything was quite literally straightened out in the end – during the very next ruck, Brown got punched again, and this time his jaw settled back into its correct position.

Brown scored eight tries in South Africa, including a try apiece in the second and third Tests. His try in the third at a time of relative parity between the sides, just before halftime, allowed the Lions to take a lead into the break that was not entirely deserved, and management were reluctant to even consider losing him. As probably the next best lineout jumper in the squad, Chris Ralston was the most plausible alternative. Under similar circumstances he had replaced Roger Uttley in the England side in South Africa in 1972 and had played an unobtrusive yet important role on the Lions' tour, playing in eight of the final ten matches, if one also considers the final Test. Considering the *snot en trane* in which South African rugby had been enveloped, this was small change. The Lions managed to confine themselves to 17 players for the four Tests, Steele losing his place to Irvine, and now Brown's indisposition paving the way for Ralston. It certainly was not the Grand Guignol bloodletting the Springboks had perfected.

Before they could run onto the Ellis Park turf, though, the Lions needed to dispose of Eastern Transvaal at PAM Brink Stadium in Springs. It was expected to be a formality, which it was, as the Lions put their sleepwalking tendencies behind them after a slow first half to win 33-10. Ralston, all of six foot six, came through the match unscathed to take his place in the second row with his skipper four days later. 'Nobody really expected Christo Holtzhausen's Easterns' side to pull off any surprises, and so it proved,' wrote *Rand Daily Mail*'s Neil Cameron. 'When the tourists put in a quick point-scoring burst in the first quarter of an hour after halftime it virtually settled the issue. But it says much for the determination of the home side that the Lions never added to the score after that and the honours in the closing minutes went to Easterns who grabbed a well-deserved try by their flank forward Klambert Fourie.'

An interested observer at the Boks' penultimate practice session on the Thursday before the final Test was Cas de Bruyn, the referee for the second and third Tests. He was a primary-school teacher in the south of Johannesburg, close to Diggers' Springfield training ground, and he took some of his pupils to watch the Boks train. He and his students were disappointed, however, because Claassen did not want to be disturbed and asked for privacy. On the field furthest away from the small Springfield grandstand, closest to the ground's perimeter fence, the forwards thundered into the scrum machine. Muller, the wing, perfected his throwing into the lineout. It was his poor throw that had been poached by Brown to give the Lions their opening try at Boet Erasmus and it was imperative that he had his communication with the recalled Williams down pat. Although Brown would be watching in the stands, the Potch professor was not going to fall into the trap of taking the dentally challenged Ralston lightly.

On an adjacent field, Ian Kirkpatrick worked with the backs. The halfback combination of Bayvel and Jackie Snyman had not yet played together in the series (Bayvel partnered Bosch in the second Test and Sonnekus partnered Snyman in the third) and they needed to become as familiar with each other as possible. Writing one of his preview pieces two days before the Test, Herman le Roux noted that Snyman was in fine form as he scooped up ropey passes from Bayvel without breaking stride. Of more concern was the flyhalf's control from the kickoff. His kicking-off had been poor in the third Test and, before the backs and forwards joined for the second half of the practice, Kirkpatrick worked on Snyman's kicking technique from the centre circle.

In the programme notes to the Transvaal game in mid-June, Rod Hartman had written an ode to Ellis Park. In it he described the old stadium's cobwebby romance – and how difficult it was to get to the press box. 'You get there by way of a devious route under the scaffolding and then up a narrow flight of wooden steps behind the main grandstand. Maybe, you might say, not the most inspiring approach to that little wooden box out of which all those volumes of words at every match flows.' Despite the fact that there were no small doors and no Queen of Hearts playing croquet nearby, the *Alice in Wonderland* feel of the press box extended to the fourth Test itself, a strangely unsatisfactory affair in which the Lions lost their bounce and the Boks finally managed to step through the looking glass towards something approaching their old selves. On a more practical note, dubious tries were allowed and apparently acceptable tries were disallowed, referee Max Baise saying many years later that he would like to be buried in the corner of Ellis Park where he awarded Roger Uttley a try that was widely felt to be marginal.

Poky as it was, on match day Ellis Park and Doornfontein, the factory-stacked suburb around the stadium, was a place of rich colours and bold contrasts. Temporary scaffolding had been erected, adding another 10 000 seats to the stadium's usual 65 000 capacity, and the day itself arrived winter crisp, warming up as kickoff approached. The clear sky was of a bright, magnetic blue, the ball was an almost buttery yellow, and the pitch was a pale biscuit colour, the winter frosts having burnt the Ellis Park kikuyu and sucked it of moisture. The teams ran on resplendent, the Springboks' gold collars bright against the emerald of their jerseys. The Lions' deep scarlet shirts looked almost menacing, attire to inspire men and frighten boys.

Baise, meanwhile, was wearing all white, except for the turn-ups of his socks. It made him more conspicuous than he might otherwise have been.

With or without its Wonderland feel, there was still continuity between the fourth Test and the previous Tests in the series. The Lions scored their tries as they always had, either from poaching or from good first-phase ball late in the game, or from exerting incredible pressure on the opposition scrum and seizing ruthlessly on the resultant panic. Their first try came from exactly this scenario: Uttley pounced on a hopeless pass from Bayvel after the scrumhalf was forced to try to clean up bad ball following a traditionally malicious Lions counter-shove, despite a Springbok feed. The Uttley try, contested by Pope and to this day disputed by most Boks and many of the South African journalists present, is as traditional a Lions set-piece as was McBride's conversation with the irate hotel manager in Port Elizabeth, a sort of spirited re-recording of one of the greatest hits for old time's sake, or Lions reprise.

If their style was stamped all over the much-disputed first try, it was also evident in the second, when the quick-witted Edwards summed up perfectly the blindside options after receiving quick ball from his number 8, Davies. Having realised that the Springbok flanks were still wedged to the rest of the pack and the blindside flanker would be unable to do his usual covering job, Edwards hared down the short side, drew his defenders and fed Irvine, who slipped past fullback Tonie Roux and sprinted over to give the Lions a 10-6 halftime lead.

While the Lions scored two first-half tries (the Uttley try was converted, the Irvine try not, Bennett's kicking form in the Test being woeful), the Springboks were by no means out of it. Jackie Snyman kept them in range with two penalties in the half. The first one was described by Gerhard Viviers in a crisp hymn to brevity. '*Dis 'n lang skop. Dis 'n reguit skop. Dis 'n oor skop* (It's a long kick. It's a straight kick. It's an over kick),' he enthused, as the Orange Free State flyhalf opened the scoring to calm the by far higher proportion of the estimated 75 000 crowd's nerves. Snyman was at it again before halftime, succeeding with his second penalty to give the Boks respectability at the break.

The Springboks not only outscored the Lions (7-3) in the

second half, but also probably had their best 40 minutes of the series since the first half of the Test at Newlands, when they turned around at 3-all. The reasons for their comparative success were various. Clearly something had worked for the pack during their two sessions against the scrumming machine at Springfield, because they were steady enough to win the tighthead count 3-1, despite being mangled by the Lions pack on the occasion of Uttley's try. Williams at lock had a fine match; the men in green winning the lineout count 29-15. Late in the game it was Williams who grabbed the ball in the lineout, controlled it and, with an Edwards-like flourish, made as if to shovel it to Bayvel. The dummy was enough to force the penalty as the Lions were caught offside; the penalty was Snyman's third, and with it the Springboks went into a 13-10 lead.

Their best moment of the Test had come just before that, when Grobler grabbed a good take from the back of the lineout and fed to Ellis. The South West Africa flanker had been sulking in the days prior to the Test, walking past the South African journos without so much as his usual relaxed greeting. Ellis had been stung by criticism – much of it mild – which dared to suggest that on the evidence of the first three Tests his best days were behind him, but here he was, initiating the pass to Schlebusch, which found its way to Pope, who scampered his way surprisingly far down the touchline before spotting Cronje roaring up alongside; Pope duly made the inside pass and Cronje collapsed over the line, a cartwheel of Lions falling with him.

Cronje was in action moments later – but on the other side of the field, playing his part in possibly the most controversial sequence of the series. A barging J.P.R. Williams's break was the main thrust of the Lions' final attacking move. After a pause it was carried on by Irish flanker Slattery, the smooth-talking lover of Beethoven and Rachmaninov, who looked as if he might have crossed the line and just got the ball down to score the winning try. Earlier, Irvine had evened matters at 13-all with the Lions' only successful penalty kick of the match. 'They were so close to our line that I realised that I couldn't go in low, so I tackled him [Slattery] high and the ball sort of got stuck between us at chest height, and it sort of wrestled down towards the ground,' remembered Cronje. 'Eventually he got it between my legs, but it depends on when Max Baise blew the whistle. Could you play the ball on the ground like that? There's no question that he got the ball down.'

In contrast to his namesake J.P.R., J.J. Williams managed to keep his temper in check on tour and was the epitome of high-minded fair play throughout. Watching his reaction to Baise's decision not to award Slattery the try is revealing. Of all of the Lions players who have chased the ball downfield and are therefore close to the action as Cronje and Slattery tumble over the line, it is J.J. who appears to be most aghast. Like those around him, he cannot believe that the try has not been awarded. It is an unsatisfactory conclusion to a series that showed South African rugby in all its parochial, self-regarding glory. Many years later, Bennett made the point that it was Baise who had to live with his countrymen. More pointedly, it was Baise who would need to serve his countrymen liquor from his bottle store in Riversdale, the pocket of the country into which he appeared to vanish. Revealingly, Baise has never appeared greatly perturbed by the Slattery mistake; rather, what bothers him is his awarding of the Uttley try. Many years later he told an Afrikaans newspaper: 'I awarded Roger Uttley's try but I was proved wrong. That's why I said that they must scatter my ashes where Roger scored because that was the biggest mistake of my life.' For his part, Uttley has come to regard the try with something less than pride. 'I look back on that with some sort of shame,' he has said, arguing that his outstretched lunge for the ball was pure instinct; that, of course, did not mean he had scored a try.

While the Boks spent their time in relative seclusion at the Taylor Travel Lodge on the Heidelberg road, the Lions, the press corps and several groups of Lions supporters stayed at the old Landdrost Hotel in the centre of town, close to what is today the Noord Street taxi rank. Everyone took their meals in Ouma's Kitchen on the first floor and the atmosphere was relaxed and amiable, players mixing with fans and both mixing with the foreign and local journalists. Le Roux remembers a group of Welsh fans mounting the stairs and singing old standbys like 'We'll Keep a Welcome' after the Test, the drinking and spinning of yarns going on well into the night. One photograph shows a group of Lions fans lying down in the hotel foyer. They have their backs on the ground and they are happily waving their feet in the air in a game of 'dead ants', a British drinking game that requires the last man to wave his feet on the call of 'dead ants' to drink a glassful of beer. Presumably one or two of these were consumed on the Saturday night after the Ellis Park Test.

The press, the fans and the historians have doggedly kept the debate about the Slattery try alive over the years (obviously slightly more so in Britain; in South Africa the stress tends to fall on Uttley's try), but the players themselves were only too happy to get together after the game. Cronje caught a lift from

Ellis Park to the Landdrost in the Lions' bus and spent much of the night in Slattery's room – or was it Uttley's? – he is not sure. After reluctantly nursing his way through one or two beers, he looked at his watch, realised he had missed the Springbok bus and wondered whether he would be able to hail a taxi at 2 a.m. on a Sunday morning. 'Late that night I found myself walking back to Randburg with my kitbag,' he recalled. 'I walked past the station up towards Jan Smuts and luckily someone stops for this guy in a Springbok blazer. I was pretty bloody relieved, otherwise I would have needed to have walked all the way home.'

This was much the way Cronje responded to life in general. Earlier in the day he had fallen asleep, as was his custom before a Test. There might have been 75 000 fans around him, baking in the winter sunshine, but he changed into his kit, propped his kitbag underneath his head and stretched out for a 20-minute kip. One of his teammates woke him up before kickoff. If only his teammates had been as relaxed throughout the series, the blundering Boks may have done slightly better.

10

Aftermath

HERMAN LE ROUX, the diligent, hard-working reporter for *Volksblad* in Bloemfontein, remembers being invited up to TRU president Jannie le Roux's suite at the Landdrost Hotel one night shortly before the fourth Test. It was a select gathering, with a handful of South African pressmen, as well as the Lions' inner sanctum: Millar, McBride and Thomas. Le Roux understood instinctively that this was no occasion to whip out the notebook. The accent was on polite conversation, a gathering of like-minded individuals discussing the game and the tour at an appropriately rarefied level. Despite all the soft cues and tacit understanding, Le Roux was unable to resist. At one point he found himself close to Millar and popped the question of the Lions scrum. The enigma had fascinated the local scribes and the South African rugby public since virtually the beginning of the tour and no one had come up with a satisfactory answer, could Millar please unravel the secret? The TRU's liaison officer, Chris Vermeulen, quietly reminded Le Roux that such questions were forbidden. He was obliged to sit down, sip his drink and chew more circumspectly on his sausage roll.

Jannie le Roux was as slick as a rat up a shithouse drainpipe, to adapt an old East Rand phrase. He had labourers working around the clock in the days preceding the Ellis Park Test to erect extra seats to extend the stadium's capacity, and his decision to rent a suite at the Landdrost for a couple of nights put him squarely in Lions territory. While Claassen and Kirkpatrick had taken the Boks off to the Krugersdorp Lion Park, where newspaper photographs show Moaner van Heerden and Tonie Roux scanning the horizon for evidence of the killer instinct they so obviously lacked, Le Roux did one better. He rented quarters in the very heart of the pride, pressing flesh and conducting himself with an urbane savvy very much at odds with the usual administrative conservatism of the day. One of the visual standbys of the period was a photograph of Craven at home in the morning, filling up a family of thermos flasks with hot water. He would schlep these flasks to work, sustaining himself through his working day with cups of tea. Le Roux was no tea drinker. He invited Millar and McBride for cocktails and saw to it that select members of the press observed the required protocols. It was not only a question of style and deportment; it was a matter of self-definition. Le Roux saw rugby as a vehicle for his moneymaking ambitions; Craven saw the sport as a select international brotherhood of Corinthian amateurs. Le Roux was never to ascend to the SA Rugby throne, but he did represent a coalition for modernisation and change. It was not one to which everyone subscribed.

While Craven and Claassen embarked on a round of pre-tour trial matches to save costs, Le Roux was, well, *making a plan*. The fourth Test earned the TRU and the SARB at least another R60 000 in revenue as a result of adding the extra seats. Le Roux was the visionary entrepreneur, while the Stellenbosch mandarins wrung their hands and counselled the increasingly beleaguered Claassen to adopt a selection policy of 'horses for courses'. Craven had been president of the SA board since 1956 and would continue to be supremo up until the cusp of South Africa's return from isolation in 1991. In 1974 he was just over halfway into his 35-year reign. It was a tour in which he covered neither himself nor those close to him in administrative glory.

In one respect, though, Craven and Le Roux were much the same – they were rugby administrators, certainly in the way players perceived them. Anton Oberholzer, the Transvaal and Diggers captain, remembers Piet Greyling, the legendary Bok loose forward, coming back to Springfield for practice one weekday evening after playing for his province the previous weekend. Greyling was incandescent with rage because Jan Lotz, one of Le Roux's henchmen, had taken exception to the players asking the union for match-day tickets for their wives. 'Lotz was *vloeking* Piet and generally treating the players like children,' recalled Oberholzer. 'I remember Piet coming back to Diggers and telling us that if he was ever spoken to like that again that he would stop playing for Transvaal and he would make sure the Diggers players never played for the province again either.'

While Craven the traditionalist and Le Roux the suave operator approached the task of administration in slightly different ways, their players were, in the main, as diligently misbehaved as players had always been. They smoked and drank and played the field, learning, as Imran Khan did many years later according to author Gideon Haig, that to swing had a slightly different connotation in the world at large to simply bowling away duckers. Bayvel, for instance, tells the story that on Sunday afternoons on tour, whether they were in Sydney or Toulouse, the Bok forwards would get out the banjo or guitar and open a bottle or two of hard tack. The backs were expressly forbidden from attending such gatherings, as many of the forwards would collapse into *dronkverdriet* complaints about one-eyed referees and the backs' life of comparative leisure. As one of the forwards, Marais remembers such gatherings well: 'I get cold shivers when I hear those stories. Frik always used to tour with his guitar and he knew a host of old *boere*-songs. Thys Lourens was often there with us and he also knew some good ones. It's a binding factor when you have demos outside your hotel howling for your blood, you get a bit drunk and sing 'Bobbejaan Klim die Berg' and 'Waltzing Matilda'. One of Frik's favourites started, "*Walvisbaai se kaal woestyne, daar drink die boere vodka en champagne* ..."'

On the Springboks' tour to France directly after the Lions tour, Bayvel was particularly impressed with Morné du Plessis' roving. Not from the base of the scrum as might have been expected, but from the team hotel when he ventured into the streets of Paris. According to Bayvel, Du Plessis disappeared some time after the post-match function one Saturday night. There was a slight raising of eyebrows when he did not appear at the breakfast table the following morning, although this should be seen in context, because almost everyone else was nursing a hangover of one kind or another. By lunchtime, Du Plessis still had not appeared and Bayvel, his roommate, began to worry. He knew Claassen would be on the prowl and figured it would probably be best for all concerned if Du Plessis, who still needed to establish himself in the side, arrived back in the early afternoon. An hour or two later, Bayvel spotted his roommate wandering into the hotel considerably worse for wear. Keeping him away from the lifts and escorting him up the stairs, Bayvel noted with alarm that Du Plessis could hardly walk. He put him to bed and hoped for the best, explaining away his absence at dinner. On the Monday morning, Du Plessis was probably worse off than he had been when he arrived back at the team hotel the day before. 'He was paralytically drunk,' said Bayvel. 'He couldn't move. He couldn't even get out of bed. I didn't know what to do because we were moving that morning. The French are clever. They don't fly you when you are playing 300 kays away, they bus you. Morné needed to get going but he wasn't moving, so I got hold of the team doctor. He travelled with a little acupuncture kit and he came round to our room. He took one look at Morné and put a needle deep and straight into the tip of his nose. Morné sat bolt upright, like he'd just received a shock, and it was enough to get him into the shower and out the door. We got him onto the bus and he slept all the way to the next town.'

Without television and its bells and whistles, like close-ups and slow-motion replays, skulduggery on the field was rife. Referees were reluctant to send players off and sanctions were minimal. The best examples of the referees' reluctance to stamp out foul play with the relish that opposing packs of forwards stamped on each other came from the Lions' games against Eastern Province and Orange Free State. Indeed, Gert Bezuidenhout, the referee in the Free State match, seemed at pains to keep players on the field. In a somewhat perverse paradox, keeping teams intact was both a way of preserving the spectacle and asserting themselves as custodians of the game. Well we remember Bezuidenhout pleading with the two teams in the Bloemfontein match to keep it clean, with a special note of desperation being reserved for his entreaties to the home forwards.

While several players I spoke to did not believe the game was any more brutal than it is today, anecdotal and circumstantial evidence suggests that the players were less self-policing and more likely to take a hack or swing a fist at an opposition player if they thought they could get away with it. Piet van Zyl, the Free State fullback, tells the story of Johan de Bruyn, the Bok lock at Boet Erasmus for the third Test, coming back to Free State practice and telling everyone that things in Port Elizabeth were 'ugly'. According to Van Zyl, De Bruyn told him 'the Bok forwards were too scared to enter the rucks' for fear of how quickly they might leave them. The game's taken-for-granted brutalities were reinforced by the fact that communication between linesmen and referees tended to be either limited or non-existent. Referees were unable to circle rucks or be on the other side of the scrum to the put-in. Without their assistants' help, they were partially blind – or at least unsighted – when it came to making decisions in certain situations and on certain sections of the field.

As the result of an accident in early childhood, De Bruyn had a false left eye. After the tour, several Lions narrated a hilarious incident in which he lost his eye in either the Orange Free State game or the third Test and the match was temporarily halted as the teams, on hands and knees, rifled through the grass trying to find it. Brown loved retelling the story and did so with relish, even giving De Bruyn the nickname 'the Cyclops'. Of the several journalists I have spoken to who saw both of De Bruyn's games against the Lions, none remembers the incident and can vouch for it. They do, however, point to a match against a French Selection XV in Lyon in November that year in which De Bruyn's eye had definitely dislodged. After a search it was found and the lock plugged it back into its socket covered in grass. 'I was playing scrumhalf that day and it happened when we took a tap-kick and Johan ran at this gigantic French lock,' Bayvel told me. 'He didn't much like him and he just wanted to run over the guy. In the tackle De Bruyn landed heavily and his false eye fell out. The French hooker took one look at this and fainted on the spot.'

Although the swings and roundabouts of forward violence tended to even themselves out in the end, some players – like Van Heerden and De Bruyn – were deemed more likely to go off than others. Sometimes the brutality needed no more justification than the fact that it was tactically expedient. Bayvel tells the story of Transvaal flying down to Cape Town for a Currie Cup match at Newlands in the early seventies. The *Rooibontes* were concerned about Dirk de Vos, the Maties and Western Province scrumhalf, who had a long dive-pass that tended to get his line away quickly and smoothly. Early in the game, after Province had won a lineout and De Vos had spirited his line away, Sakkie Sauermann casually trotted over to where De Vos was lying and trod on the back of his ankle.

'It was dirty in those days, don't let anyone tell you otherwise,' Bayvel reminded me. 'I remember in one match – a trial maybe – that Jan Ellis kicked Morné in the cheek and broke it. Morné just carried on playing. In 1976, against the All Blacks at Newlands, there was a loose scrum and Peter Whiting broke off the scrum and Moaner took his ear off. He quite literally kicked half his goddamn ear off. Ian Kirkpatrick [the All Black] had a go at Moaner for it and Moaner just sort of shrugged his shoulders as if to say: "What are you going to do about it?"'

The Lions were absolutely brutal. One of the side orders to the banquet of success has been to reframe their dastardliness. They had won the campaign, doing what no other Lions side to South Africa had done before, and one of the spoils of victory was to construct the narrative of their success in whichever way they saw fit. The mythology that has grown up around the tour has emphasised that their decision 'to get their retaliation in first' was a predictable response to past injustices. But how real these slights and injustices were can never be accurately judged – a player like Marais, for example, was seldom dirty and Ellis, for the most part, was straightforwardly virtuous.

More likely a player like Slattery would climb into an Eastern Province forward without the player having the slightest idea of what was happening. Brown and Windsor revelled in the rough stuff. J.P.R. Williams actively sought to knock people out, sprinting considerable distances to throw a punch. For all of this, there was something winningly urbane about their malice, slyly civilised as it was. It is not difficult to imagine the gent Slattery sipping a cup of tea and talking about, say, Alan Paton, while tripping a Bok as he thunders by. They were certainly a clever, streetwise bunch who knew how to push the envelope. For the most part, the South African referees allowed them to get away with as much as they pleased.

Edwards's gamesmanship, for instance, was legendary. He could often be found nibbling away at the referee's resolve: witness the game against Orange Free State in which he insisted on a substitute bringing on a doctor's note. The tourists' manipulation of referees and gamesmanship were such issues by the end of the tour that Herman le Roux even wrote an article about it, detailing the many shades of the Lions' palette. Did the referees realise, for example, that in the tight early game against South West Africa, Edwards did not, in fact, touch down, but such was the jubilation from his teammates that the partially unsighted referee wrongly assumed a try had been scored? And why was the perpetually chatty Slattery never asked to shut up? Or Edwards for that matter, who was never shy to point out an infringement in the scrum?

Still, the referees and the board only had themselves to blame. They could have insisted that Slattery and others stop their shirt-tugging; they could have policed the lazy running and the subtle creep offsides; they might even have had conversations with people like Millar and McBride. But none of this appeared to occur to them and may not have done any good anyway.

As the tour progressed, and the Lions' first series win in South Africa became a possibility, the likelihood of doing anything to compromise already fragile relations became increasingly remote. From a distance, the referees appeared to be terribly eager to please. In many ways they were as intimidated as the South African players themselves, which in a small way probably contributed to the Lions' growing self-confidence as they trawled through the Republic.

11

Edward Heath's cheesy smile

WHEN THE LIONS arrived in South Africa, they did so under the long shadow of official disapproval. They returned to Britain to have many of the same people who had criticised them when they departed seek them out and congratulate them – an irony that was not lost on the group. Edward 'Teddy' Heath, the former prime minister, was on hand to smile for the cameras with McBride and Brown, and McBride made sure that the furry lion the Lions had *schlepped* around South Africa was on hand to experience his moment in the glare of Heath's beneficent smile. Denis Howell, the then Labour minister for sport, was also at Heathrow that sunny English day to press flesh and have his say. He opens his self-exculpatory justification by using the words 'I thought it only right …', which indicates that he was not blind to the limitations of his position. It also suggests a decency lurking beneath the opportunism, one which, in effect, says: 'We realise we're looking a little stupid now but we still thought it best to be seen to be offering our congratulations. We understand that some will interpret it as expedience.'

The question of whether or not it was prudent to travel to southern Africa never quite went away, but it was certainly softened by the fact that the Lions returned home victorious. For those of a liberal inclination, the Lions' tour demonstrated, yet again, that sportsmen are largely self-serving when it comes to factoring broader political issues into their lives and adjusting their behaviour. Then again, the players' views on such issues cannot summarily be dismissed. Winning in South Africa would be one of the pinnacles of their careers. Being preached to by anti-apartheid protesters and Labour politicians, many of whom they did not much care for anyway, was scandalously beside the point. While they instinctively recoiled from being dictated to – the set-piece meeting of McBride and Hain in the reception area of the Britannia Hotel at the beginning of the tour is an object lesson in mutual incomprehension – we should not be too quick to dismiss the players as unfeeling.

Many of the Lions were bothered by the iniquities of apartheid South Africa. Still more were horrified by the obvious gulf in living conditions and opportunities. Understandably they took some degree of refuge in the fact that they were in the country to play rugby, although some, like Slattery, ventured off the beaten track to investigate the pockets and dark recesses behind the informal *cordon sanitaire* of receptions, trips to Kruger and five-star living in the best hotels. Despite this, we should be slightly suspicious of, say, J.P.R. Williams's claims that the tour contributed to apartheid's decline ('Many of us felt that if we could beat the Boks we could help the system to change,' he wrote in his autobiography), which have a slightly self-serving ring to them. Rather than contributing to apartheid's decline, what the Lions did was to help change South African rugby. This is not nearly as relevant or socio-politically sexy as giving apartheid the finger, admittedly, but the Lions helped to drag

South African rugby out of the Dark Ages, which itself led to a general argument about the value and necessity of integration, firstly in the rugby sense, secondly in the more general sense that there were certain advantages to being citizens of the world.

Strange as it might sound, the British Lions did South African rugby a favour by touring. This was because in beating the Boks – and remaining unbeaten for as long as they did – they demonstrated unequivocally that South African rugby was in a proudly backward phase. The mandarins and Stellenbosch visionaries, ordinary coaches like Diggers' Jim Foley, had allowed South African rugby to drift away from its traditional strengths. How many times did someone like Syd Millar say, while on tour, that as a younger player he had learnt so much about the centrality of the scrum from South African rugby? South African back play was now sclerotic, there was little to choose between functional but limited scrumhalves, and the flyhalf cupboard was so bare it echoed long and hollow. More difficult to quantify but of equal importance was the fact that South African rugby had lost self-confidence. Without anyone really noticing, the debate had become how to keep the Boks in the international game, rather than what was happening in the game itself. So *verskrik* were the administrators about isolation, about the political implications of apartheid politics, that they failed to notice the technical and intellectual adjustments and changes that had swept through British rugby. Whether these took the form of the Welsh coaching revolution or the natural competitiveness of a tough competition like the Five Nations, the South Africans, as perhaps befitted their status as folk of the distant veld, did not seem in the slightest bit interested.

Hain might have seemed a colourful irrelevance in 1974,

having yet to reach the stage where he was demonised as white South Africa's enduring pet hate. But being a boy from the suburbs of Pretoria, he understood something fundamental about the white South African psyche – the importance of sport to their self-definition. Towards the end of the tour, Albert Agar, then secretary of the British Home Unions, was invited to watch the last Test as a guest of the SA board. When interviewed in the local press, Agar made the point that although provision had been made for a Lions tour of South Africa in 1980, he doubted very much that it would come to pass. As the opinion of one influential man, it should not be taken as representative of the broader consensus, but Agar was not hopeful. He did slightly contradict himself, however, because during a function in Durban between the third and the fourth Tests he said that, by the same token, international rugby bosses were not predisposed to being dictated to by men with 'long hair'. So much for the grandeur of ideas. This one was about bedrock prejudices and matters of style: the cut of one's blazer, the length of one's hair and the colour of one's politics.

The dislike of those with long hair won out in the end, because a Lions side did come to South Africa in 1980, and generally international rugby, unlike international cricket, was slow to shun South Africa. Hain was clearly wrestling with a foe more obdurate than he envisaged, although he will point to the fact that between 1980 and 1997 the Lions did not tour the beloved country at all. Finally, the lessons handed down by McBride's clan were rugby ones, not moral or political ones, and there is reason to believe that such lessons were learnt and imbibed quickly. There is nothing quite like washing down your medicine with the draught of shame and humiliation. The Boks did not like it, but there is reason to believe that they swallowed hard and got on with it.

*

The sparkling paradox – indeed, the try-scoring moment – for the 1974 Lions was that their time in the African sun coincided almost perfectly with the slope of their decline. Millar and McBride's forward-orientated template was so successful in South Africa that it was widely adopted by the four Home Unions. The game became highly efficient from a technical point of view, but possibly unnecessarily dour in Britain as a result. British rugby lost sight of the rounded game that had served them so well in New Zealand in '71 and, to a lesser extent, in South Africa three years later. The backs and running play in general were marginalised, as coaches adopted what might slightly facetiously be called the 'Millar and McBride matrix'. John Reason caught the paradox almost perfectly four years after the '74 tour in *Lions Down Under*, his book about the Lions' next tour, to New Zealand in 1977, a series they lost.

'The [1977] international season in Europe had confirmed that British forward play was becoming ever stronger and better organised, technically more efficient and physically more prepossessing,' he wrote. 'Unfortunately, it had also confirmed that British back play had ebbed to the lowest point in its history. No world class players had emerged in Britain behind the scrum since JPR Williams and David Duckham had first played international rugby in 1969. The problem [of poor midfield play by the Lions in 1977] was aggravated by the disastrous devaluation of the back play which was the consequence of the nine-man rugby played by the 1974 British Lions in South Africa. ... The fact remains that in four short years [since 1974], British back play succeeded in becoming stereotyped.'

In a roundabout way the widespread adoption of the matrix was a vindication of sorts for players like Gibson, Duckham and Gerald Davies. Unlike the other two, Gibson did, of course, tour, although he was not chosen originally and flew out later. They might have mouthed the correct sentiments in justifying their absence, but British rugby historians (and punters at the time) have long suspected that the three knew which way the Lions coin was going to fall once Millar and McBride had been appointed. There was certainly a tactical pragmatism to the Lions because, when the opportunity arose at places like Loftus Versfeld for the second Test and Boet Erasmus for the third, they were prepared to run to the point that they scored eight tries in two Tests. They might have scored nine, given that they fell inches short when the final whistle was blown in Port Elizabeth, but the fact remains: their domination of the Springboks was predicated on their technical superiority over the Bok front five. The Lions won the set-pieces and the collisions. They won their own scrum ball and were brilliantly destructive of the opposition's, frequently compromising apparently decent ball or just turning it plain bad.

For their part, the Springboks, the selectors, the administrators and some of the fans simply sulked. Certain individuals retreated to the farm, as did Marais in times of stress, to nurse endless cups of coffee and stare at the aloes on top of the *koppie*. For the most part, the sulks were short-lived, but some curdled into something deeper, something close to a kind of millennial guilt, as was the case with Claassen. When I asked him whether he could recall any light-heartedness or any moments of levity in those long winter months, he replied: 'The best part of the tour by far was when the Lions packed up and went home.'

Despite the sulks and the pockets of morbidity, the establishment managed to find some chipper part of their collective selves. They had a tour of France later that year to prepare for and Andy Leslie's All Blacks were hoped-for tourists in 1976. It is moot as to how good either side really were. New Zealand rugby was struggling to come to terms with the ramifications of their '71 Lions defeat, and a workmanlike Ireland side lost 3-11 to them in June 1976, shortly before Leslie's side flew to South Africa. The French, as always, were in the midst of one of their protracted guillotine moments – chopping and changing with apparent alacrity. Jean-Pierre Rives was a standout performer when France beat England 27-20 at Twickenham in the 1975 Five Nations campaign, but was not by any stretch of the imagination a shoe-in for the French side at the time. Having beaten England 'sublimely', according to Griffiths, they could barely sneak past Scotland in Paris (10-9 to France) and were beaten in their final fixture of the Five Nations' calendar that season by a mediocre Ireland in Dublin. Rives played no part in either South African Test in 1975, with the seven new caps for the Bloemfontein Test suggesting that the French selectors were behaving in a startlingly similar way to the Springbok selectors of the previous year.

No one minded the standard of the opposition, because South African rugby was in no mood to quibble. The wins against France away in the latter stages of '74 and at home in the winter of the following year were lapped up with a mixture of relief and old-fashioned Springbok arrogance, the complacent assumption being that the Boks had rediscovered their *cojones* and returned to their old ways. It was not always as easy as it seemed, however. Marais, for example, found the trip to France in '74 stressful, particularly as he had to take over the coaching of the side because the old warhorse Claassen was forced to come home because of illness. 'It took us four Tests against the Lions to work out our best side, and we only used 16 players for the Tests against France later that year and that, I can tell you, was a very decent French side,' Marais said. 'I could have kissed Ian Kirkpatrick when he stepped off that plane to come and take over after Prof had gone home. I had to take training and captain the side, so it all became a bit of a challenge.'

The individuals in the Bok establishment who genuflected most at the altar of shame were the older men – Marais and Claassen. Marais, I sensed, felt particularly aggrieved. He had not expected to play international rugby again and only accepted Claassen's invitation out of decency and a sense of honour as a former Springbok captain. His fate was to not only lose the Eastern Province captaincy in controversial (and possibly unfair) circumstances, but also to lose the series in humiliating fashion. He was blessed, though, by his dignity and what was essentially a down-to-earth goodness. The Lions respected this and he was never forgotten, being invited to all the tour anniversaries, where he was honoured and made a fuss of. This is not to say that regret did not gnaw at him. It took a long time for the sharp edges of his disappointment to soften, which is how we should understand his decision to continue playing after the series was lost.

Although Claassen is a more naturally remote man, he was better able to articulate his sense of shame and failure, and better able to excavate the emotions layered beneath the surface. In several things he said he implied that the series defeat was a trauma from which he took years to recover. This was said matter-of-factly, without self-pity or accusation and, as such, it had the ring of truth. There was only one series – either as a coach or a player – that bothered him deeply, and the Lions tour in '74 was it. 'It is the only Test series [in which] I was guilty,' he said. 'I was the chairman and our policy of picking [players] was wrong.' In the same interview he compared his challenges to the challenges faced by St Paul after he saw the light on the road to Damascus. 'To find truth in a broken world is a challenging, challenging job. To be a Springbok coach and selector in a broken world isn't quite the same, but nearly,' he told me.

Such were the man's trials and the way in which he made sense of them. What struck me most about Claassen through all of this was his nobility. I have heard stories about the infamous Bok tour of New Zealand in '81, when Claassen shied away from media duties and ran away from journalists who were prying and confused. On the way home from New Zealand there was the Test in Chicago against the USA Eagles that nobody knew about, and Claassen, much to the journalists' chagrin and frustration, pretended it was not happening. In his dotage, sitting in his khaki flannels and dark Oxford shirt, his tastefully ordinary herringbone tweed, he is not the same man who inspired the kind of fear so many young players of the time spoke about. I can see how he could have been intimidating; I can see that he protected himself in the aura of what a Springbok coach should do and how he should behave. For all this, his acceptance of guilt, his willingness to be held accountable and his long wrestle with the consequences of his decisions strike me as acts of uncommon decency. 'We realised very early there is a lot to do,' he told me. 'You can't blame the internal situation and the politics. If you wanted to play international rugby, you had to play up to standard. We didn't do that.'

Without too much imaginative difficulty I am able to think of rugby in South Africa in almost elemental terms, as something natural rather than cultural, as something which seeps so deeply into our sense of self and nation that it functions like water or air. Men like Claassen have something to do with that, as well as men like Marais and even men like MacDonald, the unlucky Springbok. What they bring to the culture and history of the game in this country is not reducible to physical courage, although that is part of it. They bring their gravitas, yes, and, as in Claassen's case, they bring their sorrow. But they also bring their tradition of valour and emotional courage that has allowed them to look back and face their past. In different ways all three have locked horns with regret.

It is not fair to compare their struggles, but Claassen seemed still burdened by his wrestle with the disappointments of the Lions tour. Marais seemed to have reached a sort of wry accommodation, not entirely comfortable, but one with compensations. MacDonald, I would hazard, still struggles with the primal unfairness of his one and only Test. In their long loneliness they have fought with the series and their part in it and reached some sort of peace. For this they are all worthy of the greatest respect.

Summary of tour fixtures and results

Date	Opponent	Venue	Score	No. of tries
Wed 15 May	Western Transvaal	Potchefstroom	59-13 (22-13)	nine tries
Sat 18 May	South West Africa	Windhoek	23-16 (10-9)	three tries
Wed 22 May	Boland	Wellington	33-6 (10-0)	five tries
Sat 25 May	Eastern Province	Port Elizabeth	28-14 (16-4)	three tries
Wed 29 May	South Western Districts	Mossel Bay	97-0 (37-0)	16 tries
Sat 1 June	Western Province	Cape Town	17-8 (11-4)	two tries
Tue 4 June	SA Rugby Federation XV (Proteas)	Goodwood	37-6 (13-6)	five tries
Sat 8 June	South Africa	Cape Town	12-3 (3-3)	
Tue 11 June	Southern Universities	Cape Town	26-4 (16-4)	four tries
Sat 15 June	Transvaal	Johannesburg	23-15 (3-9)	three tries
Tue 18 June	Rhodesia	Salisbury	42-6 (25-6)	six tries
Sat 22 June	South Africa	Pretoria	28-9 (10-3)	five tries
Thurs 27 June	Quaggas	Johannesburg	20-16 (13-7)	three tries
Sat 29 June	Orange Free State	Bloemfontein	11-9 (4-3)	two tries
Wed 3 July	Griqualand West	Kimberley	69-16 (25-3)	12 tries
Sat 6 July	Northern Transvaal	Pretoria	16-12 (9-6)	two tries
Tue 9 July	SA African XV (Leopards)	Mdantsane	56-10 (17-3)	10 tries
Sat 13 July	South Africa	Port Elizabeth	26-9 (7-3)	three tries
Wed 17 July	Border	East London	26-6 (10-3)	three tries
Sat 20 July	Natal	Durban	34-6 (9-0)	four tries
Tue 23 July	Eastern Transvaal	Springs	33-10 (16-6)	five tries
Sat 27 July	South Africa	Johannesburg	13-13 (10-6)	two tries

Abbreviations and acronyms

BBC: British Broadcasting Corporation
FHUC: Four Home Unions Committee
IRB: International Rugby Board
SAA: South African Airways
SABC: South African Broadcasting Corporation
SAPA: South African Press Association
SARB: South African Rugby Board
TRU: Transvaal Rugby Union
UCT: University of Cape Town
WRU: Welsh Rugby Union

Glossary

babbelas: hangover
bliksem: strike or punch
bloed-Sap: a diehard member of Jan Smuts's South African Party
boere: farmers
boerewors: sausage
die groot kanonne: the big guns
die saai lewe: the dreary, humdrum life
dronkverdriet: maudlin drunkenness
gatvol: fed up
groot gemors: big mess
immigrante: immigrants
jol: a good time
klap: slap or smack
koppie: hillock
koshuis: boarding house
kwaai druk: intense pressure
maagspiere: abdominal muscles
mielieboere: mielie farmers
moer in: hell in
moerse: huge
padkos: food for the road
platteland: rural country
Rooibontes: Transvaal rugby players, nicknamed for the red hoop on their white jerseys
snot en trane: misery, literally snot and tears
sterk manne: strong men

stuk: piece
swartbordrugby: blackboard rugby
tjoepstil: very quiet
verskrik: frightened
vloeked: sworn at
vloeking: swearing or cursing
volstruisboere: ostrich farmers
vrot: rotten
wenrugby: winning rugby
windgat: boastful

References

Bryant, John. *3:59.4: The Quest to Break the 4 Minute Mile*. London: Hutchinson, 2004.

Coleman, Nick, and Nick Hornby (eds). *The Picador Book of Sportswriting*. London: Picador, 1996.

Craven, Danie. *Die ABC van Rugby*. Johannesburg: Janssonius & Heyns, 1966.

———. *Doc Craven's Tribute: The Legends of Springbok Rugby, 1889–1989*. Howard Place: KC Publications, 1989.

Greyvenstein, Chris. *Springbok Saga: 100 Years of Springbok Rugby*. Cape Town: Don Nelson, 1989.

Griffiths, Edward. *The Captains*. Johannesburg: Jonathan Ball, 2001.

Haigh, Gideon. *On Warne*. London: New York: Simon & Schuster, 2012.

Hain, Peter. *Outside In*. London: Biteback Publishing, 2012.

Lister, Simon. *Supercat: The Authorised Biography of Clive Lloyd*. Bath, England: Fairfield, 2007.

McBride, Willie John (with Peter Bills). *Willie John: The Story of My Life*. London: Portrait, 2004.

McLauchlan, Ian. *Mighty Mouse: An Autobiography*. London: Stanley Paul, 1980.

Partridge, Ted. *A Life in Rugby*. Johannesburg: Southern Book Publishers, 1991.

Reason, John. *Lions Down Under: The 1977 British Isles Rugby Union Tour of New Zealand and Fiji*. London: Rugby Books, 1977.

——— (ed.). *The Lions Speak*. London: Rugby Books, 1972.

Thomas, Clem, and Geoffrey Nicholson. *Welsh Rugby: The Crowning Years, 1968–1980*. London: Collins, 1980.
Williams, J.P.R. *JPR: An Autobiography*. London: Collins, 1979.

Newspapers
Die Burger
Daily Dispatch
Daily Telegraph
Eastern Province Herald
Natal Witness
Rand Daily Mail
Rapport
The Star
Sunday Times
Volksblad

Television documentaries
Glorious Victorious
The Invincibles
A Pride of Lions
SA Mirror

Index

Do you have any comments, suggestions or
feedback about this book or any other Zebra Press titles?
Contact us at **talkback@zebrapress.co.za**

*

Visit **www.randomstruik.co.za** and subscribe
to our newsletter for monthly updates and news